10
Millie Bobby Brown
Facts

Mera Wolfe

Contents

Introduction

Think you know everything there is to know about about Millie Bobby Brown? Well, think again. 1000 Millie Bobby Brown Facts contains all you could ever wish to know about this teenage superstar. Facts about Stranger Things, fashion, family, likes & dislikes, food, career, background, Enola Holmes, lifestyle, famous friends, Godzilla, quotes, awards, sneakers, beauty products and so much more all awaits in 1000 Millie Bobby Brown Facts.

Facts

(1) Millie Bobby Brown was born in Marbella, Spain, in 2004 to British parents.

(2) Millie was born on the cusp of Aquarius and Pisces but says she relates more to Pisces.

(3) Millie was born with partial hearing loss and is deaf in one ear.

(4) Millie has a brother named Charlie and two sisters named Paige and Ava. One sister is younger and one is older. Charlie is nearly ten years her senior.

(5) When she was four years-old, Millie's family moved back to England from Spain. They spent some time living in Dorset (on the south coast) and in London.

(6) Millie's old primary school teacher later said she always knew Millie would be very famous one day. Millie went to Pokesdown Community Primary School in Bournemouth, England.

(7) Millie's family eventually moved to Florida in the United States to start a business. Millie was around eight years-old when this happened.

(8) When her family moved to Florida, Millie took part in some local acting workshops because she was bored at the weekends and wanted something to do. She was patently a natural and a Hollywood talent scout told her family they should move to Los Angeles so Millie could pursue an acting career.

(9) Millie's first ever audition was for a Publix commercial. Publix is a chain of supermarkets in the United States. "I went

in there and I had no idea what I was doing," said Millie. "I was really boring. And then I had to hold cupcakes and say like, "Mom can I please have some chocolate chip cupcakes," or something like that. And the guy actually grabbed my face, and then grabbed my hand and pulled me out of the audition and then said, "Where is your father?" "Where is your mother?" And started looking at all the parents and my dad was like, "Uh, I'm her dad." He was like, "She's got the job, she's got the job." And I was like, "Okay, okay." And like immediately I got the job. I was immediately happy and I was just very content and blessed. Like immediately I knew that I was just born to do this."

(10) Millie said that when she began going for auditions in the United States she eventually pretended to be American to boost her chances of success.

"I was always prepared, but they rejected me because I was English. For this reason, at a certain point, I decided that I would pretend to be an American: as soon as I got the role, I started talking again with my British accent. They looked at me in amazement and I'd be like: 'Too late, the contract is signed!'"

(11) Millie never went to a regular school again after she left England and was home-schooled thereafter. This means that her education took place at home with private tutors and her parents.

(12) Within weeks of becoming a fledgling child actor, Millie took the part of young Alice in ABC's Once Upon a Time in Wonderland (which was a spin-off from Once Upon a Time) . Sadly though this wasn't a recurring role (Millie was only in two of the thirteen episodes that were eventually produced) so it didn't last very long. Millie's dream was to be a regular in a television show because that way she would be guaranteed work.

(13) In 2014 Millie was cast in the spooky BBC America drama

show Intruders. The main actors in this show were John Simm and Mira Sorvino. In the show, Millie played a little girl who is used by a serial killer to house his spirit. Sadly though, Intruders only ran to eight episodes and did not perform well enough to earn a second season.

(14) The famous horror author Stephen King singled Millie out for praise on Twitter when he watched Intruders. He said that Millie was one of the best child actors he had ever seen. This was quite ironic because a few years later Millie would become world famous for her role in a show that was heavily by King's horror fiction.

(15) Millie's other early acting roles were in the procedural drama NCIS, the sitcom Modern Family, and the medical drama Grey's Anatomy.

(16) Millie has trained in Thai boxing and ju-jitsu.

(17) Millie said her worst audition was for a Barbie commercial. "It was very awkward," Millie said. "It was hard. I had to jump up and down. They gave me this, I don't even know what it was, it was just this thing I had to hold and stand up and play pretend with this other girl."

(18) Millie auditioned for the part of Laura/X-23 in the Hugh Jackman film Logan but lost out to Dafne Keen. Millie said she did her audition in front of Hugh Jackman - which was a great experience even if she didn't get the part. Millie has praised Dafne Keen's performance in the film.

(19) Millie tested for the part of the little girl Sophie in Steven Spielberg's film adaptation of Roald Dahl's The BFG. The part went to Ruby Barnhill in the end though.

(20) In 2015, Millie won her famous role when she was cast as Eleven in Stranger Things. Stranger Things is a Netflix sci-fi horror show set in the 1980s.

(21) Millie said she nearly quit acting before she was cast in Stranger Things so it was very lucky that she kept going in the end and didn't give up.

(22) In the first season of Stranger Things, Eleven is a girl with telekinetic powers who escapes from a government laboratory and helps three boys on their quest to find their missing friend Will Byers. The government agents and scientists held Eleven captive because they wanted to exploit her super powers to help them fight the Cold War against the Soviet Union (the first season of the show is set in 1983). After she escapes, Eleven is given secret shelter in the basement of a boy named Mike Wheeler.

(23) Over 300 girls auditioned for the part of Eleven before Millie was cast in the role.

(24) Millie did an initial Skype audition for Stranger Things in London with an impeccable American accent - which she taught herself by watching the Disney channel. This impressed the casting director.

(25) Millie had no idea in her Stranger Things auditions that Eleven was going to have super powers nor that she would be playing a major character in the show. Millie would later say she had assumed Eleven was going to be a minor sidekick.

(26) Millie's auditions for Stranger Things were made up of special scenes created solely for her screen tests.

(27) Millie said she had to do several auditions for the part of Eleven. In the end she was flown to Los Angeles for more screen tests. At this point she deduced that she must be quite close to getting the part if they were taking the time and expense to fly her across the Atlantic.

(28) The Duffer Brothers (who created Stranger Things) found that Eleven was the hardest character to cast in season one of the show. The main reason for this is that child actors often

find it hard to stay in character when they don't have any dialogue and have to stay silent. The Duffers saw that Millie was clearly able to sustain the same level of focus at all times - even with the very minimal dialogue of Eleven.

(29) Millie thinks that her ability to cry convincingly as an actor was one of the salient factors in her casting as Eleven. Eleven spends a lot of season one crying!

(30) Millie had to play scenes with various boys who were in contention to play Mike Wheeler during the Stranger Things casting process. When she played a scene with Finn Wolfard and had excellent chemistry with him the casting department knew they had found their Mike Wheeler.

(31) Millie said that at her Stranger Things audition she was asked about the eighties movies she had watched. Despite her tender years Millie proved to be surprisingly knowledgable when it came to classic films made before she was born.

(32) Before she was famous, Millie used to have her own YouTube channel in which she sang covers of popular songs.

(33) Millie was required to shave her long hair into a military buzzcut to play Eleven in season one of Stranger Things but cheerfully accepted this condition in the end. She was shown a picture of Charlize Theron in Mad Max: Fury Road to see what her hair was going to be like in the show.

(34) In the original plan for Stranger Things, Eleven was going to have no hair at all. In the end they gave her more of a Jean Seberg crop.

(35) Millie only found she had to shave her hair to play Eleven after her final audition when she was offered the part.

(36) Millie is friends with Maddie Ziegler. Maddie Ziegler became famous as the girl dancing in Sia's music videos. Maddie Ziegler had never heard of Stranger Things when she

became friends with Millie so she binged the show to see what all the fuss was about.

(37) Millie says her dream role is to play the young Princess Leia in a Star Wars film. Many have noted her resemblance to a young Carrie Fisher.

(38) Millie was - appropriately enough - eleven years-old when she played Eleven in the first season of Stranger Things.

(39) Millie is the youngest person ever to feature on the Time 100 list of the 100 most influential people.

(40) The character of Eleven famously loves Eggo waffles but Millie, who is English, wasn't au fait with Eggo waffles at all and neither were her family. "Eggos are an American thing," said Millie, "and my British family is like - We don't know what that is!"

(41) Millie said she was mistaken for a boy a few times when she had her buzzcut to play Eleven in season one of Stranger Things.

(42) Millie isn't really a big fan of Eggo waffles in real life.

(43) Millie said if she was forced to eat some Eggo waffles she would pick the blueberry ones.

(44) Millie says she would love to be in a musical film one day.

(45) The cast of Stranger Things bonded very quickly on season one. The children, who aside from Gaten Matarazzo and Caleb McLaughlin had never met before, all became close right from the start. Noah Schnapp (who plays Will Byers) and Millie in particular became best friends.

(46) Millie invented Eleven's head-flick and 'magician's wave' for when Eleven deploys her powers in Stranger Things.

(47) Because the part of Eleven mostly requires a very internal and controlled performance (with precious little dialogue), Millie loves any scenes where Eleven has to shout or scream.

(48) Millie was the youngest person to reach 20 million followers on Instagram.

(49) Millie does strength conditioning each day to stay in shape.

(50) Millie says she likes junk food but only in moderation.

(51) At the time of writing, Millie has 46 million Instagram followers.

(52) Millie said she never googles herself and that her social media is all run by her family.

(53) When the first season of Stranger Things was a big hit in 2016, Millie and the other kids in the cast went out trick or treating at Halloween. Their costumes must have been very good though because no one deduced who they really were.

(54) Millie is a fan of the Burberry fashion brand.

(55) in the first ever episode of Stranger Things, Millie's character Eleven had to eat some strawberry ice cream when she ventures into a diner looking for food. Millie didn't enjoy this scene because she doesn't like strawberry ice cream very much. "We were on set, and they asked what flavor I wanted," said Millie. "I told them I prefer light vanilla, but I asked what looks better on camera. Little things like that make a difference. They said strawberry. Ugh, that is my worst flavor. I asked the question, didn't I? So I was like OK. Fine. I ran to my trailer green. I wanted to vomit so badly."

(56) Millie was named the number one breakout star of 2016 by IMDB.

(57) Millie unsuccessfully auditioned for a part in the 2016 film The Boss. Millie was tested to play the young version of Melissa McCarthy's character. The part went to Isabella Amara.

(58) Millie did not enjoy shooting the scene in the season one finale of Stranger Things where Mike kisses Eleven. At only eleven years-old, Millie found that kissing (even on the cheek) wasn't tremendously appealing. She is said to have declared that "kissing sucks" afterwards - which amused the crew.

(59) Millie was something of an overnight sensation when season one of Stranger Things came out. At the tender age of twelve, Millie was soon being offered modelling contracts, magazine covers, interviews, convention appearances, music videos, and movie roles.

(60) Millie said she didn't like shooting the scenes where Eleven is alone in Hopper's cabin in Stranger Things 2. She didn't like being apart from the other actors.

(61) Millie and the other children in the Stranger Things cast had to arrange their education around the production and were assigned tutors and a classroom on the set.

(62) Millie said that on the set of Stranger Things she likes to have her trailer next to Sadie Sink's trailer. Sadie Sink joined the cast in season two.

(63) Millie is the youngest ever Unicef goodwill ambassador.

(64) In their interviews for Stranger Things 2, the Duffer Brothers said that Millie is always game to do multiple takes of a scene to make it absolutely perfect.

(65) Millie has done a shoot for Calvin Klein.

(66) When it comes to Sneakers, both Eleven and Millie seem to like Converse. Millie has done commercials for this brand.

(67) Millie is a big dog lover and her family have always had several dogs.

(68) Millie and Noah Schnapp pranked the Stranger Things costume designer on season one by pretending that she'd had a phone call saying her wedding venue was double booked.

(69) The character of Eleven is full of allusions to Jean Grey in The X-Men. The specific arc is the Dark Phoenix saga by Chris Claremont and John Byrne that collects X-Men #129-137. Will suggests in the first episode that X-Men #134 should be the prize in a cycle race with Dustin. The telekinetic Jean Grey loses control of her powers in this comic arc and becomes the terrifying Dark Phoenix. The X-Men must try to both stop and save her - which is no easy task given how powerful she is.

The sequence in season one where Eleven loses control of her powers in the lab and overloads the system (thus creating the breach between dimensions) is a very obvious reference to Jean Grey becoming Dark Phoenix. There is a scene in the Wheeler house too where Eleven notices a small trophy of a winged woman. This is another reference to Jean Grey.

(70) Millie said she was scared of the dark growing up and slept with twinkle lights around her bed.

(71) Eleven's blonde wig in season one of Stranger Things was, believe it or not, worth $8,000. Millie hated wearing the wig because it made her head itch in the warm weather. Sometimes the fashion department would find the wig hanging from a tree after Millie had taken it off and completely forgotten about it.

(72) When they made season one of Stranger Things, the Duffer Brothers (jokingly) described Millie as a forty-one year-old Shakespearean actress trapped in the body of an eleven year-old girl.

(73) Millie said she loves eating Ramen noodles after a busy day acting because they don't take long to cook.

(74) The nosebleeds suffered by Eleven in Stranger Things are not CGI but practical effects. A fake corn syrup blood solution is syringed into Millie's nose.

(75) During production on the first season of Stranger Things, Millie turned up on the set one morning covered in gold glitter. It had be removed before she could do any scenes.

(76) Millie said she's more scared of ghosts than the Demogorgon monster in Stranger Things.

(77) Millie said her Instagram followers spiked in amazing fashion when season one of Stranger Things came out. "I was actually in a car on my way to San Francisco. I didn't even watch it when it came out. I just saw my Instagram followers going up every second. I went from 25 to 1.4 million – pretty cool."

(78) Millie has appeared in four music videos.

(79) Millie was involved in UNICEF's #GoBlue campaign for World Children's Day.

(80) Millie said the attention to detail on Stranger Things is so precise that the costume department even supply 1980s underwear.

(81) Millie is 5'5 in height and apparently still getting taller.

(82) Millie is a supporter of Liverpool football team. In 2016 she visited Anfield stadium and was given a special Liverpool shirt by the club with 'Millie' printed on the back. "When I was younger, my dad got me a whole Liverpool kit," said Millie. "My brother is a massive fan and it's kind of like a legacy. I didn't really have a choice! Now I watch them and I love Liverpool."

(83) Millie said that because her hearing is quite poor, they have to have someone next to her say action when she does a scene. "At a young age, I've always had bad ears and never really could hear anyone. But filming Stranger Things was hard because I would have to have ADs or PAs near me to say action because they'd have to say it really loud or make a sign so I could watch them, because I would never be able to hear them."

(84) Millie was signed by IMG models in 2017.

(85) Millie was involved in an EA Games collaboration for The Sims.

(86) Millie not only played the title character in the movie Enola Holmes but was also one of the producers. She was only fifteen years-old at the time!

(87) Millie said she had never encountered a record player before she went on the set of Stranger Things for the first time. She liked them so much though she got one for Christmas.

(88) Millie had to wear a Sea Trek helmet and descend into a water tank for real to shoot the scene where Eleven enters the sensory deprivation water tank in the lab for Dr Brenner in season one of Stranger Things. Her helmet was equipped with a radio through which the Duffer Brothers could talk to her.

(89) Millie wears some Reebok High Top White Sneakers as Eleven in Stranger Things 3.

(90) Millie is a fan of Stella McCartney fashion.

(91) Millie has displayed her talent for rapping twice on the Jimmy Fallon show.

(92) Millie has done a fashion campaign for Moncler.

(93) After season one of Stranger Things was a big hit, Millie and some of the cast visited the White House and found that President Obama was a big fan of the show.

(94) Millie only says 246 words as Eleven in the first season of Stranger Things.

(95) Of the main characters, Millie is the second youngest cast member in Stranger Things. Noah Schnapp, who plays Will Byers, is the youngest as he was born six months after Millie.

(96) Millie, despite only being eleven years-old, was completely unphased by the dark and frightening scenes she sometimes had to play in season one of Stranger Things. As soon as the scene was over, she was back to singing pop songs and cheerfully chatting away to the crew. It was the complete opposite of method acting.

(97) Millie said of her personality - "I can be rebellious. But not so much. I've never been grounded by my parents. I'm a very good girl. But I do believe in making noise, in being loud!"

(98) Millie said she likes the vanilla latte from Starbucks.

(99) Millie said at Asia Comic Con the story that her father started crying when she had her long hair shaved to play Eleven is not true. She said it was her mother who got upset.

(100) Millie says that the kids in the Stranger Things cast often play board games to pass the time between takes.

(101) Millie said her family made a lot of financial sacrifices to facilitate her acting ambitions.

(102) Before she became famous through Stranger Things, Millie auditioned for the role of Lyanna Mormont in Game of Thrones but lost out to Bella Ramsey. Millie said she was devastated not to get this part.

(103) Millie said she would seek sanctuary in Winona Ryder's trailer when the boys got too annoying during the production of season one of Stranger Things.

(104) Millie said she is a big fan of Jodie Foster. Jodie Foster also began her career as a child actor.

(105) Millie said she lost her voice no less than five times shooting Stranger Things 3 because of all the screaming that Eleven does.

(106) Eleven was originally supposed to be killed off for good at the end of the first season of Stranger Things. The Duffers altered their plans when they saw how great the character was and how great Millie was. A second season of Stranger Things sans Eleven became inconceivable.

(107) Millie said that when she's in England she watches the daytime magazine shows Loose Women and This Morning.

(108) Millie said she is scared of bungalows! She said she finds the concept of a house with no upstairs rather disconcerting.

(109) Elizabeth Wagmeister, a senior correspondent at Variety, called Millie one of the biggest child stars in the history of Hollywood.

(110) Millie has a dimple on her right cheek.

(111) Millie Bobby Brown said she didn't know anything about Godzilla before she was cast in Godzilla: King of the Monsters. "I'll be honest, I was definitely not a fan of Godzilla, which is a good thing because my character isn't. My character is just a teenage girl who's just learning. She's learning about Godzilla and the titans as she goes along. She doesn't really know how she feels about him."

(112) Millie's dad said - "Millie is all confidence and swagger in the world, but at night, at home, she can turn into a little, shy

girl. It's a side of her that only her family sees."

(113) Millie signed-up to support girls' and women's soccer as an ambassador of UEFA's Together #WePlayStrong campaign. "I've grown up playing football with my family and we are all are huge Liverpool fans," said Millie, "so I was really excited when UEFA approached me to join the squad. What I love about Together #WePlayStrong is its values: they're not only centred around football but also friendship, building confidence, teamwork and equality.

Kicking the ball around with the girls was really cool and fun. It felt great to be part of a team that has such a strong sense of unity. Even though it felt a little intimidating to join in on a football session for the first time in a while, I had so much fun and would encourage any girl thinking about trying the sport to just give it a go."

(114) Millie said she loved the fact that Eleven was one of the most popular Halloween costumes of 2016. She said that if anyone knocked on her door in an Eleven costume at Halloween she would definitely give them some candy.

(115) Millie says she would love to make a comedy film one day. "I definitely want to do a comedy because I think I am very funny. I've done many dramas already that I'm ready to explore other things."

(116) Netflix did not disclose the salaries of the cast but it was widely reported that Millie was the highest paid of the child actors in Stranger Things 2.

(117) Millie says her lucky number in real life is not eleven but eight.

(118) Millie is a fan of Nicki Minaj.

(119) Just prior to production on season two of Stranger Things, Millie was asked in an interview about Sean Astin

(who is famous for The Goonies and The Lord of the Rings) joining the cast and seemed completely confused. Millie clearly had no idea who Sean Astin was and didn't know he had joined the show!

(120) Linnea Berthelsen (who played Kali in one episode of Stranger Things 2) found Millie to be very professional and wise beyond her years when they shot The Lost Sister. Berthelsen noticed how Millie would even make suggestions to the director.

(121) It was Millie's idea for Mike and Eleven to kiss in the Stranger Things 2 finale.

(122) Millie is a fan of the late Amy Winehouse.

(123) Millie has her own beauty line called Florence by Mills.

(124) Millie was nine years-old when she began her acting career.

(125) At the time of writing Millie has an estimated net worth of $10 million.

(126) Millie loves Jolly Rancher candy. She likes sour cherry the best.

(127) Millie appeared on Gordon Ramsay's Hell's Kitchen when she was ten years-old. She wasn't very famous at the time.

(128) Millie said that the thing she misses the most about England is a nice cup of tea with some digestive biscuits.

(129) Millie said the colors she likes best are blue and white.

(130) During the production of Stranger Things 2, a fan infiltrated the set and got a picture taken with Millie.

(131) Millie said she especially enjoyed playing Eleven in season two because she got to display more emotion in comparison to season one.

(132) Millie is a fan of rock climbing.

(133) Millie watched some classic eighties movies to prepare for Stranger Things. She said she especially enjoyed E.T and Stand By Me.

(134) The Duffer brothers, inspired by Japanese manga, first conceived Eleven as a much more violent character. The version of Eleven we see in Stranger Things does kill - but not to the extent that the Duffers originally planned.

(135) Stranger Things was going to be called Montauk when Millie did her audition. Montauk is a hamlet at the east end of the Long Island peninsula. The Duffer Brothers eventually decided though that they didn't want the show to be set in Montauk so they had to change the name and came up with Stranger Things.

(136) Millie has won the award for Best Dramatic TV Performance at the IGN People's Choice Award.

(137) Millie and the kids in Stranger Things started their own chat group called Stranger Texts.

(138) David Harbour (who plays Hopper) said Millie and the kids were highly amused by the 1980s telephones when they saw the Stranger Things sets for the first time.

(139) Some movie buffs have pointed out the physical similarity between Tami Stronach as The Childlike Empress in The NeverEnding Story and Millie as Eleven. Millie met Tami Stronach at a convention.

(140) The child extras at the Snow Ball dance finale (where Mike and Eleven kiss) in Stranger Things 2 were not told that

they were appearing in Stranger Things and so it came as a nice surprise to them when the penny dropped.

(141) Michael Dougherty, the director of Godzilla: King of the Monsters, said they always had Millie as their top choice to play Madison. "Part of my process for writing a script involves doing screen grabs or image searches of actors or actresses you think would be great in the role and Millie Bobby Brown was the person we thought of for Madison,"

(142) Millie is one of the youngest people ever to be nominated for an Emmy. Six-year-old Keisha Knight Pulliam for The Cosby Show was the youngest.

(143) Millie said she has a strong work ethic but wouldn't like to be thought of as a workaholic. "I'm not obsessed with it, just because that would be unhealthy, but I definitely love working and keeping myself busy and learning new things."

(144) Millie got her part in the BBC America show Intruders without even meeting the producers. They cast her on the strength of her audition tape.

(145) Millie is a fan of Italian food.

(146) In 2020, Millie donated $18,000 to three hospitals on the south coast of England where she used to live. Millie said - "Britain's NHS (National Health Service) workers -- and all carers -- are an inspiration to us all and are the nation's heroes. I am in awe of every one of them and just wanted to thank those risking their lives - particularly in hospitals on the South coast. The area is very dear to me and my family and I cannot wait to visit again soon. Keep up the brilliant work and stay safe. Thank you. You are all amazing."

(147) Millie said that when she made Enola Holmes she drank Lucozade in the morning to keep her energy levels up.

(149) After season one of Stranger Things came out, Millie was

asked which character she would choose to rescue if she could only pick one. Millie picked the Byers family dog Chester.

(150) Millie says she is a big fan of salads. Caesar salad is the one she likes the most. A Caesar salad is a green salad of romaine lettuce and croutons dressed with lemon juice (or lime juice), olive oil, egg, Worcestershire sauce, anchovies, garlic, Dijon mustard, Parmesan cheese, and black pepper.

(151) After Stranger Things 2 was released, Millie's Instagram followers jumped from five million to 15 million.

(152) Millie said that when she was shooting season one of Stranger Things, after she finished her scenes she would sneak back onto the set to watch Winona Ryder act.

(153) Millie said she has secretly stolen some socks from the Stranger Things costume department!

(154) Comics Beat wrote of Enola Holmes - 'The charm of Enola Holmes lies not just in Millie Bobby Brown's enchanting performance, though it captivates almost immediately and viewers quickly fall in love with her repartee and individualism. The charm also lies in Jack Thorne's screenplay that mixes the earnest with the humorous and adds a healthy dash of adventure. Thorne blends a classic bildungsroman with a mystery that is worthy of even a great detective like Sherlock Holmes.

Enola is certainly a perfect choice for a leading protagonist in contemporary times. She is independent, brave, intelligent, curious, and stubborn. She stands out as easily as she can blend into a crowd. She's depicted as having an intellect that matches and even exceeds her famous brother. Time and time again, she is forced to make difficult decisions and she makes the choice with both her head and her heart, something that keeps her apart from her colder brothers and even her mother.'

(155) Millie said that, although she is English in real life, it was rather strange to play Enola Holmes because she was only used to acting with an American accent.

(156) Stranger Things casting director Carmen Cuba said of Millie's audition - "An agent who knows my taste very well sent me info on her and I was intrigued so we had her tape. She's based in London so she taped herself and it was amazing — really emotional and intense, lots of tears — and that's where we started with the process.

From there, we had her do additional material, gave her some direction over email, and eventually, Skyped with her then brought her to the US to test with our other kids. She did the entire Skype in an American accent and it was so good we didn't even notice until the very end. Millie was very impressive on all levels."

(157) In the pilot script for Stranger Things, Benny's Burgers was going to be a fish and chip diner. The fact they didn't do this must have been a relief to Millie because the pilot script had a scene where a starving Eleven bites the head off a raw fish in Benny's diner!

(158) Millie said when she went to get her driving permit she was - spookily enough - number eleven on the waiting list.

(159) When the first photos from the set of Stranger Things 2 emerged, Millie was conspicuously missing. The Duffer Brothers and Millie were vague about whether or not Eleven was returning at first in order to make her return more of a welcome surprise. This ruse didn't really fool anyone in the end and Millie's presence on the set and in publicity photographs was soon apparent. No one seriously believed they were going to make a second season of Stranger Things without the biggest breakout star of the first season! That clearly would have been mad.

(160) Millie's skin and makeup range is vegan.

(161) Millie earned one million dollars for starring in Godzilla: King of the Monsters and also got a share of her character's merchandise sales.

(162) When shooting Stranger Things 3, Millie was told to save her biggest screams for the end of major scenes so she wouldn't lose her voice too much.

(163) Millie said she always has guacamole in her fridge. Guacamole is an avocado-based dip.

(164) Millie is a big fan of the actress Lily James.

(165) Millie said that Mothra is the monster she likes the best in the Godzilla universe.

(166) The yellow Polly Flanders inspired dress that Eleven wears in season one of Stranger Things (when the boys dress her up to go to the school and use the ham radio) took a long time to find. It had to be a special dress because why would Nancy have saved it otherwise? There were several versions of the yellow dress made because it had to appear progressively dirty and worn the longer that Eleven wore it.

(167) Millie said she is a fan of the Twilight movie series with Kristen Stewart. Millie admires Kristen Stewart as a versatile actress who has done many different things.

(168) The Duffer Brothers said that a lot of networks rejected Stranger Things because they didn't think a show with children as major characters would work. The networks were obviously completely wrong about this.

(169) It took Millie and the kids two days to film the Snow ball dance scenes at the end of Stranger Things 2.

(170) The overnight fame Stranger Things bestowed on most of the cast was something that some embraced more than

others. Millie seemed to be having the time of her life whereas the very private Natalia Dyer (who played Nancy Wheeler) said she had taken to wearing a hat in public so she wouldn't be recognised. It's probably fair to say that Millie is more extrovert than Natalia.

(171) Millie loves churro. A churro is a fried-dough pastry based snack.

(172) The Duffer Brothers said they had already decided to team up Millie and David Harbour in season two of Stranger Things even before season one had ended. In season two, Hopper rescues Eleven from the woods and eventually adopts her.

(173) It was Kimberly Adams who had the clever idea of dressing Millie (as Eleven) in Finn Wolfhard's Mike Wheeler's clothes when she hides out in the basement of the Wheeler house in season one of Stranger Things.

(174) Eleven is not really supposed to be a fashion savvy girl so Millie is never dressed in what you would describe as high fashion in Stranger Things.

(175) Millie that when she bumped into Caleb McLaughlin (who plays Lucas in Stranger Things) again for the first time after having her hair shaved to play Eleven he had no idea who she was at first because she had very long hair when she first met him.

(176) Millie said it is more difficult to play a part that doesn't have much dialogue - like Eleven in Stranger Things. "I find it more difficult than actually having [a lot of] dialogue. Because if I have dialogue, I'm more focused on the dialogue. But with my actions, you know, I have to cry sometimes, and even if I don't have to cry, I well up because she's so emotional."

(177) Concerning the sensory deprivation water tank scene in the lab in season one of Stranger Things, Millie said it was very

difficult to scream in a diving helmet while underwater!

(178) When Millie appeared on breakfast television in the United Kingdom after Stranger Things came out, viewers were very surprised to discover she was English because her American accent in Stranger Things had been so convincing. Most people had assumed Millie must be American in real life too.

(179) Millie claims she has never watched a Marvel film. She said they aren't really her cup of tea.

(180) Millie has said she is a big fan of scary films.

(181) Millie said she watched a lot of episodes of Friends during the COVID lockdowns.

(182) Millie says she likes arts and crafts as a hobby.

(183) Millie says she is not a slave to technology and thinks she could survive without a cell phone.

(184) Millie said her perfect snack is carrots with hummus. Hummus is made from cooked, mashed chickpeas blended with tahini, lemon juice, and garlic.

(185) Millie's mother apparently has to approve what she wears onscreen to make sure it is appropriate for her age.

(186) Millie was reportedly paid $20,000 an episode in the first season of Stranger Things. She would get a huge pay rise in future seasons.

(187) When she was told the premise of season one of Stranger Things, Millie asked the Duffers why Joyce Byers didn't contact her missing son Will Byers on his telephone. Millie was unaware that people didn't carry mobile telephones around with them in 1983.

(188) Millie said she loves the scent of Lavender.

(189) Millie says she is team Stancy when it comes to Stranger Things. She wants Nancy Wheeler to end up with Steve rather than Jonathan.

(190) Millie's salary for Stranger Things 3 was said to be a mystery. Many entertainment sites speculated that she was now being paid as much as the adult leads like David Harbour (who was said to now be on $350,000 an episode). Although these sound like high figures, they were not outrageous by television standards. In 2004, the six leads in the popular sitcom Friends were all paid one million dollars per episode - and that was for 18 episodes.

(191) Kimberly Adams, the Stranger Things costume designer on season one, said of Millie - "I loved working with Millie Bobby Brown. Not your typical 11 year-old, an old soul! She brought so much to that character."

(192) Millie said she would like to write and direct in the future.

(193) Millie is a fan of the singer Adele.

(194) Finn Wolfhard can be seen whispering a warning to Millie before Mike kisses Eleven in the Stranger Things 2 finale.

(195) Epsom salt (in huge quantities) was used to float Millie in the season one Stranger Things sequence where they create a sensory deprivation water chamber in the school. All the salt gave Millie a headache.

(196) Millie said she took home two props from the set when season one of Stranger Things finished production. Some of the fake blood (for Eleven's nosebleeds) and Eleven's fake 011 tattoo.

(197) Millie estimated that she only had to eat the equivalent of a couple of Eggos shooting season one of Stranger Things. Her character Eleven was obviously depicted eating a lot more than that.

(198) Millie is a fan of Beyonce.

(199) Millie deleted her Twitter in 2018 after being the victim of homophobic memes by idiotic trolls with nothing better to do.

(200) When it comes to food, Millie said she loves a good chilli con carne.

(201) Good Morning America wrote of Enola Holmes - 'Stranger Things star Millie Bobby Brown, who just turned 16, shines her talent on its highest beams in Enola Holmes. The British actress plays the title role, the kid sister that Sherlock Holmes -- Man of Steel Henry Cavill, no less -- never really had in the classic fictions of Sir Arthur Conan Doyle. My advice when watching this is: Just go with it, since Brown is totally irresistible and brings a cool vibe to this family entertainment.

Based on the first book in a six-book series by Nancy Springer, the film adapts the same style its director Harry Bradbeer used in Fleabag, in which Emmy winner Phoebe Waller-Bridges talked directly to the camera, meaning to us. It's an old trick, but Brown gives it a fresh spin that works like a charm. Meanwhile, the action hurtles in every direction, sometimes creating a jumble the turns logic into the film's missing link.

Luckily, Brown stays dazzling as Enola outsmarts Sherlock and battles Mycroft for sending her to, ew, finishing school. Cavill underplays nicely as Sherlock, letting the detective's droll tolerance of his sister grow into grudging admiration. Purists didn't mind when Robert Downey, Jr. and Benedict Cumberbatch energized the Holmes mystique with their modern takes, so why kick now just because a fiercely independent teen girl is bringing a millennial zing to the Holmes mystique? Note to Netflix: Get busy making the films of the other Enola books. And if a young-adult audience, charged by seeing Brown in the role she was born to play, wants to shout, Enola Forever, it's about time.'

(202) Millie deployed some method acting for the scene at the end of Stranger Things 3 when Eleven reads Hopper's letter from beyond the grave (though in reality we knew that Hopper was likely to return in Stranger Things 4). Millie only read the letter for the first time when she did the scene and the emotion of the writing was sufficient to make her tear up.

"They had prerecorded David [Harbour] and they played it out loud," said Millie. "I didn't want to read that speech. I didn't want to hear about it. I didn't want to rehearse it. I just immediately wanted to put a camera on me and find the way I react and the way I reacted was pure devastation and sadness, and a distraught child that just lost her father or so she thinks. So it was definitely a raw emotion, especially because David Harbour and I are really close. He is just one of the greatest men. I think something I admire about David is he respects girls and women so much. It felt so... I'm so gutted and I was like, 'Oh, my God, this is horrible.' So the emotions were raw in that scene for sure."

(203) Millie is friends with some of Angelina Jolie's children.

(204) Millie thinks she is quite sarcastic in real life. She thinks her wit is occasionally quite dry and English.

(205) Millie's production company is called PCMA Productions.

(206) Millie has appeared in commercial advertisements for Citigroup.

(207) Millie said she is scared of sharks.

(208) For Eleven's nosebleeds in Stranger Things, the red corn syrup mixture has to be injected up Millie's nostril and she then has to tilt her head back to keep it in place until the nosebleed is supposed to happen.

(209) Millie's hairstyle and some of her clothes in Stranger Things 2 were based on a cover illustration for the 1981 children's fantasy book Ronja Rövardotter by Astrid Lindgren. The illustration depicted a farm girl in the woods with curls in her hair.

(210) When Millie is acting in something her older brother Charlie is usually on the set to look after her.

(211) Millie is said to have earned six million dollars to appear in Enola Holmes.

(212) The character of Eleven was partly inspired by the manga series and anime Elfin Lied. Elfen Lied is about a girl who has telekinetic powers and escapes from a military facility.

(213) Millie said she didn't act in anything at school in England and has never been in a play. Millie said that if she was in a play she'd be worried she might sneeze and ruin a scene!

(214) Millie thinks that Dr (Papa) Brenner in Stranger Things isn't as bad as he seems.

(215) When Stranger Things 2 came out, Millie performed a Stranger Things season one recap rap on The Tonight Show.

(216) Stephen King's Firestarter is one of the most obvious influences on Stranger Things and the character of Eleven. Firestarter revolves around a young girl who has pyrokinetic abilities because her parents were subject to MKUltra type experiments when they were teenagers. It is possible that the Duffers were inspired specifically by the 1984 movie version of

Firestarter. There are many concepts in Firestarter that Stranger Things uses - like the girl (named Charlie) suffering nosebleeds and wearing electronic sensors on her head to monitor her during lab experiments. The film starred Drew Barrymore - who was one of the biggest child actors of the 1980s. Drew Barrymore interviewed Millie a few years ago for a magazine.

(217) Millie said she likes romantic films most of all.

(218) Millie says she has suffered from anxiety. "I struggle with anxiety and in some ways, this has hindered it. When I'm having a bad day or I'm feeling very anxious, some things like when people say, 'Oh, you looked bad at this award show because you looked like this or you looked like that,' make me a little bit more anxious."

(219) Millie was nominated for the 2018 Emmy Award in the Supporting Actress in a Drama Series category for her role as Eleven in Stranger Things.

(220) Natalia Dyer (who plays Nancy Wheeler) and Millie use the same stunt double in Stranger Things.

(221) The costume department on Stranger Things say they have to be careful not to dress Eleven in anything too fashionable because otherwise she ends up looking more like Millie Bobby Brown the celebrity actress rather than the character of Eleven.

(222) Millie said she didn't like the fact that Mike and Eleven broke up during Stranger Things 3 and was relieved that they reunited in the end.

(223) Millie won the Choice Breakout TV Star award at the 2017 Teen Choice Awards.

(224) Millie said she would like to own a farm one day.

(225) Many people have said that Natalie Portman looks like a grown up Millie Bobby Brown. Portman played Eleven in a Stranger Things skit on Saturday Night Live and met Millie in real life. "I had met Millie at the Golden Globes a few months ago." said Natalie Portman, "and she came up to me and was like, 'People keep telling me I look like the kid version of you!' I see that there's something there, but I also find her, like, much more magical than I see myself. She's really wonderful."

(226) Millie said she finds it difficult to contemplate life beyond Stranger Things. "I don't want to think about life after Stranger Things. It makes me too sad. They're like my family."

(227) When she was asked what happened to Eleven at the end of season one of Stranger Things (Eleven mysteriously vanished in a cloud of dust after battling the Demogorgon), Millie (with her tongue in her cheek) said - "Eleven goes to LA, you know, she has a super famous boyfriend. She lives in a mansion, she forgets about Mike, you know, who is he?"

(228) Millie passed her driving exam in 2019.

(229) Hopper reads Anne of Green Gables to Eleven in the cabin in Stranger Things 2. Anne of Green Gables is a classic 1908 children's book by L M Montgomery. The story concerns the adventures of Anne Shirley, an 11-year-old orphan girl.

(230) Millie says she loves being by the beach.

(231) Eleven's longest phrase in season one of Stranger Things is only seven words long.

(232) Millie said she has never watched a Harry Potter film.

(233) Millie said she was a Hannah Montana fan as a kid.

(234) Millie said it was very uncomfortable wearing a Victorian corset to play Enola Holmes.

(235) Millie has joked that because she has to travel so much she often feels as if she lives on an aeroplane.

(236) Millie said she wore pajamas everyday during the COVID lockdowns.

(237) Millie said she likes Filipino food.

(238) Millie said she has always been a drama queen and threw a lot of tantrums as a child.

(239) Because Stranger Things is based in Atlanta, Millie spends a lot of time living in Georgia.

(240) Psychokinesis or telekinesis (the power that Eleven has in Stranger Things) is an alleged psychic ability allowing a person to influence a physical system without physical interaction.

(241) Millie used to have a punching bag in her garden for workouts.

(242) Millie says she loves the 1980s and thinks it would be fun to live in that decade.

(243) Millie said her family keep her feet on the floor because she isn't allowed to act like a celebrity at home.

(244) The scene in the first ever episode of Stranger Things where Eleven ventures into Benny's diner searching for food was not a pleasant experience for Millie. "Oh, that was the worst day in the world!" said Millie. "I had to stuff my face with cold fries. They were so greasy. I had like three burgers, and I'd put them in my mouth, and they were cold. I was like, are you kidding me? I had a cup beside me and then I would spit the burger into the cup and come back up. There's a blooper take where I just spit it right out. Everyone starts laughing."

(245) Millie said - "I want to try controversial roles. Something that really challenges me. Not that everything I've done wasn't challenging. It was. I definitely want to try something that takes preparation, that takes studying. If it's a movie about someone and I'd be playing that someone, I'd love that. I want to be versatile."

(246) Millie's English accent threatened to break through occasionally shooting season one of Stranger Things. Whenever this happened they had to do another take.

(247) Although the character of Eleven doesn't say much, Millie has more screen time in Stranger Things than any other character.

(248) The Eleven Funko Figure is naturally holding a box of Eggo Waffles.

(249) Gaten Matarazzo (as Dustin Henderson) carrying Millie (as the exhausted Eleven) into the classroom in the finale of season one of Stranger Things was impressive because Gaten had an injured ankle at the time.

(250) At at a comic con after Stranger Things 2, Millie was asked who she would save out of Hopper and Mike if she could only pick one. Millie chose Hopper because she felt Finn Wolfhard wouldn't be too bothered by her choice but David Harbour on the other hand would be devastated if she didn't choose Hopper!

(251) Millie's hair obviously grew considerably after season one of Stranger Things was produced and so for the scene in the second episode of Stranger Things 2 (where there is a flashback that takes place right after Eleven has confronted the Demogorgon in the first season finale) CGI had to be used to give the impression that Eleven still had her famous buzzcut.

(252) Eleven bleeds from the left nostril when she uses her powers.

(253) Eleven appears to be bleeding from the wrong nostril in one of the Stranger Things season three posters.

(254) Millie said she is a big fan of The Walking Dead. The Walking Dead, like Stranger Things, is set in Atlanta so Millie has met some of the cast.

(255) The Duffer Brothers say that Millie will sometimes listen to music to prepare for an especially emotional scene in Stranger Things.

(256) Millie said Noah Schnapp had a mishap on the set of Stranger Things 2 when he got stuck in a chair!

(257) In the Stranger Things 2 scenes where Eleven is a fugitive living in the woods, some sunburn cream was put on Millie to give her a cold and frozen glaze.

(258) Millie was nervous about a new girl joining the cast of children in Stranger Things 2 in case they didn't get along. Happily, she quickly became friends with Sadie Sink and these fears proved unfounded.

(259) Kim Wilcox was the costume designer on Stranger Things 2. Wilcox was in charge of Millie's punkish change of image for The Lost Sister.

"What I wanted to do was find something that would be slightly more pop culture but still punk," said Wilcox. "If you remember in the '80s, Madonna was famous for wearing these blazers, rolling up the sleeves and popping the collar. Madonna stole that from the punks, so it's kind of a hand-me-down already. We definitely tried a few different kind of jackets on and this was the one that definitely spoke the most to us. It made a lot of sense for her.

The thing about that jacket is it feels a lot older than it is. We needed something that we felt like, in the '80s, when you were looking in the thrift store and your parents' closet, the things you thought were cool was from the '60s. So if you were thrifting, that's what you would pick. So we wanted something that actually felt much older than the '80s, but that would make sense for her."

(260) Millie as Eleven is always the focal point of the official Stranger Things poster art.

(261) Millie said that saying goodbye to the catering department after Stranger Things 3 finished production made her cry. "Saying goodbye to the people who make my food, I mean, seriously. That's the people I live off of, quite literally!"

(262) Millie had to do some wire work for some of the Stranger Things 3 action sequences scenes and suffered from dizziness as a consequence.

(263) Millie said that hardly anyone has Netflix in the quiet part of Georgia she lives in - so as a consequence no one knows who she is because they don't watch Stranger Things.

(264) Millie is a fan of of the singer Ed Sheerhan.

(265) When they did their first ever press interviews for Stranger Things, Winona Ryder and Millie genuinely seemed to have no idea if there would be a second season when they were asked about the show's future. At that point no one really knew because they were waiting to see how the show would be received.

(266) When production on Stranger Things 3 ended, the cast were allowed to do some free shopping in the Starcourt Mall set (which was built into a real defunct mall). Millie filled up a bag of goodies from the Gap store. Saidie Sink didn't have much luck though because she left her bag of goodies in her trailer and forgot to take them home.

(267) Millie said one of her toughest scenes in Stranger Things

3 came when the monster grabbed Eleven's legs and she had to scream while upside down!

(268) Eleven, when used with a capital E, translates to elf in Dutch or German.

(269) The platform that Hopper and Eleven descend on (when they have to close the dimensional gate) in the Stranger Things 2 finale had to sway around and this left Millie feeling seasick.

(270) It is estimated that Millie's character Eleven might have killed as many as twenty people during the course of the first three seasons of Stranger Things!

(271) Millie said her favourite movie is the Pixar film Up.

(272) Millie's salary on Stranger Things 3 netted her $2.7 million for the entire season. This was a huge pay increase from what she earned on previous seasons - especially season one.

(273) Although she doesn't like sharks, Millie is a big fan of whales.

(274) Millie said that internet trolls do not bother her. "I honestly actually feel really bad for them because who knows what they're going through," she said.

(275) Of the four boys in Stranger Things, Millie said in 2016 - "The boys have their squads. They have their group, and it's definitely difficult because they're boys and talk about boy stuff. They talk about girls and video games. I definitely need to talk about normal things a girl would talk about. They're like my big brothers. They annoy me, but we are very, very close."

(276) Millie said that the toughest scene for her in Stranger Things 2 was when Eleven encounters an apparition of Matthew Modine's Dr Brenner. She said she had to dredge up

a lot of emotion to play this scene.

(277) Millie said her dad cried when he watched the first season of Stranger Things. She was very pleased that all the drama had an emotional effect.

(278) When it comes to auditions, Millie said - "I think I was quite accustomed to it. I knew what the industry was about-I knew that it was competitive. I had best friends who were in the industry, and I'm like, it's cool if you get a job, and I'm happy. Before an audition, I'm like, "Good luck," I really am. So I think that it's important just to stay humble and really not make it a competition. It's about the art and you're being a participant."

(279) Millie said she always gets emotional when she takes off her 011 tattoo for the last time when production on a season of Stranger Things ends.

(280) Millie said she suffered from some bullying when she went to school. "I was bullied at school back in England. I actually switched schools because of it, it created a lot of anxiety and issues that I still deal with today. I have dealt with situations both in real life and online that are soul-breaking and it genuinely hurts reading some of the things people have said."

(281) Sadie Sink thinks her real life friendship with Millie makes the friendship between Max and Eleven all the more believable in Stranger Things. "Max makes friends with El this season. Me and Millie, on weekends, we'd have sleepovers and stuff – I think that's why our onscreen relationship came across as very genuine, because of how close Millie and I are. Being the two girls on-set, we had this automatic bond. It could have been a really bad situation or something, there could have been jealousy: "Oh, there's a new girl." But it wasn't, because me and Millie just really get along."

(282) Elizabeth Wagmeister said that history is littered with

child stars who fell by the wayside when they became adults but she believes that Millie has the talent and savvy to avoid this pitfall. "She proved that she is wise beyond her years and can remove herself from a situation, instead of giving into the drama. At a very young age, Millie has shown that she knows how to create her own narrative, rather than letting Hollywood write it for her. At the end of the day, we have not seen any reason for concern with Millie. Her team seem to be navigating her career very smartly. The key to success for child stars is playing a variety of parts to show range without jumping to adult roles too quickly."

(283) In the original pitch booklet for Stranger Things, the notes on Millie's character Eleven are - 'Eleven was an orphan with telekinesis. Her preternatural abilities have been linked to genetic mutations caused by her mother's drug use. When she was just two years old, she was taken for experiments by a clandestine faction of the U.S. Military. She has subsequently lived out a majority of her life in a small cell beneath Camp Hero.

During this time, she and a group of other children (One to Ten) were subjected to a series of painful, dangerous experiments. Her powers proved greater than the other children, and she began to receive special attention from Agent One. Outside of Agent One, she has little experience interacting with others and has no memory of the outside world. When she escapes the laboratory at the start of our series, she finds herself experiencing real life for the first time. This proves both terrifying... and thrilling. If Mike is the Elliot of our show, Eleven is our E.T.'

(284) Millie said she finds it a bit strange to see grown men cosplaying Eleven.

(285) Sadie Sink and Millie asked the Duffer Brothers to make Max and Eleven best friends in Stranger Things 3 because they wanted to have more scenes together.

(286) Millie said shaving her hair off for the part of Eleven was strangely empowering. "The day I shaved my head was the most empowering moment of my whole life. The last strand of hair cut off was the moment my whole face was on show and I couldn't hide behind my hair like I used to."

(287) After the kiss between Mike and Eleven at the Snow Ball dance in the Stranger Things 2 finale, the extras all gave Millie and Finn Wolfhard a round of applause.

(288) Millie Bobby Brown said she was very proud to become the youngest Unicef goodwill ambassador.

"With fame comes a lot of negative and positive aspects. But one of its good aspects was my becoming a goodwill ambassador for Unicef. It's a platform I can use to spread an amazing message, because I like empowering the youth. Now, I can support children's rights and help young boys and girls fulfill their dreams and get what they deserve—like education, clean water, vaccines, home for their families and a safe place to be. These are things I'm passionate about—and, luckily, Unicef has made all of that possible."

(289) Millie and Sadie Sink became such good friends making Stranger Things 2 they went on a family holiday together when shooting ended.

(290) Millie said it was genuinely emotional shooting the scene at the end of Stranger Things 3 when Joyce Byers moves out of Hawkins with her kids and Eleven.

(291) Matthew Modine said he was quite shocked by the glee and delight of Millie at shooting the scenes in season one of Stranger Things where Eleven kills government agents!

(292) Millie said - "On a set I don't want to be treated as a minor, although I am, I am not there to just be treated like a child, I am there to be treated as a co-worker and my opinion be treated as such. I am a girl but that doesn't matter, our

opinions are equally as important as each other."

(293) Millie said she was very nervous on the set of Godzilla: King of the Monsters because she'd never done a film before.

(294) Despite her youth, Millie has already appeared on dozens of magazine covers.

(295) Millie says she would much rather have avocado toast for breakfast than Eggo waffles. She says though that she is not a big breakfast person and can't always face food first thing in the morning.

(296) Eleven's character in season one of Stranger Things is a well worn trope in fantasy films. She is someone who is special but, because of extraordinary circumstances, doesn't understand the normal everyday world and finds it confusing. Examples of this trope include (obviously) E.T, but also the artificial boy in D.A.R.Y.L., Johnny Five in Short Circuit, Madison the mermaid in Splash, and Jeff Bridges in Starman.

(297) Eleven's hair in season one of Stranger Things could be an Alien 3 Easter egg. Sigourney Weaver shaved her hair for the film because her character Ripley lands on a prison planet that has a big problem with lice.

(298) Millie was recovering from a fractured kneecap early on in the production of Stranger Things 3 season three and therefore restricted in what she could do. She had to have a double fill in for her in the scenes where Eleven and Max ride bikes.

(299) Although Millie was separate from the boys for most of season two in her scenes as Eleven, she saw them on the set all the time because they had their school classes together during the production.

(300) You can purchase an Eleven nose bleed candle in which you put a red candle in a candle holder of Eleven's face (which

doesn't actually much resemble Millie
if truth be told) and then when the candle melts Eleven has a
nosebleed. This item is quite hard to find now - which
probably isn't a great loss.

(301) Millie has said she loves to watch the Kardashians.

(302) The famous 2013 video game The Last of Us features a
little girl named Ellie. Given the Duffer Brothers great love of
horror and post-apocalyptic video games it wouldn't surprise
you if Eleven's name was inspired by a game.

(303) Millie said she ate some mint tic tacs before she had to
kiss Finn Wolfhard in the Stranger Things 2 finale.

(304) The kids (now teenagers) in Stranger Things are given
relatively little makeup because the Duffer Brothers think it is
more realistic if they have a few spots and blemishes.

(305) The salt needed to float Millie in the kiddie paddling
pool sensory deprivation scene in season one of Stranger
Things equated to 24 bags of salt.

(306) 37% of Millie's lines in Stranger Things 2 come from The
Lost Sister alone. The Lost Sister is an unusual episode
because it shone a solo spotlight on Eleven and didn't really
feature the other regular characters.

(307) Although he is one of her best friends, Millie says she
doesn't like having her trailer next to Noah Schnapp on the
Stranger Things set because he's too loud and makes it
impossible to take a nap.

(308) Stranger Things casting director Carmen Cuba said of
Millie Bobby Brown - "I don't think anyone could predict the
kind of superstar she would become because none of us
imagined the show itself would get the kind of attention that it
did. I did think from the start that she was a deeply talented
actress and that she had the potential to be someone who did a

lot of amazing work in the future."

(309) Millie and Noah Schnapp became best friends through Stranger Things but - much to their frustration - their characters Eleven and Will Byers barely say a word to one another in the first three seasons of Stranger Things.

(310) Millie is a big fan of the actress Felicity Jones.

(311) Millie said she would love to play a zombie in The Walking Dead.

(312) Although the cover of the book Ronja Rövardotter by Astrid Lindgren was cited as the main influence for Millie's hair in Stranger Things 2, one might argue that she also has a similar hairstyle to the one Sigourney Weaver had in the classic movie sequel Aliens. Stranger Things 2 is rife with Aliens references so this might not be a coincidence.

(313) Millie's ability to stay in character with laser guided focus even without dialogue is illustrated perfectly in the season one Stranger Things scenes where the kids hide out in the junkyard bus. Dustin paces up and down - all nervous energy and anxiety - and constantly mutters to himself and yet Eleven is completely calm and self-contained and even cuts him a small bemused look as if she doesn't understand how anyone can be so emotional and chatty. It's what you might describe as a brilliant piece of 'background' acting.

(314) Millie said she enjoyed going home to England to make Enola Holmes.

(315) In 2020 it was reported that Netflix had offered Millie a lavish deal in which would have the pick of future projects to star in.

(316) A sequel to Enola Holmes has been given the green light.

(317) Millie said she would like to see Mike and Eleven get

married at the end of Stranger Things.

(318) Millie said she loves to get her nails done but unfortunately all her nail art has to come off when she plays Eleven in Stranger Things.

(319) Millie said that when you are a celebrity you have ignore most of the ridiculous whispers and untruths you attract because you can't respond to everything.

(320) Enola Holmes was not released in cinemas because of COVID. It was still very successful though and was streamed 76 million times in the first four weeks it was available,

(321) Movie Web wrote of Enola Holmes - 'Enola Holmes has a primary theme of female empowerment. Enola is constantly underestimated because of her sex and youth. She disguises herself to move freely in different situations. But she also makes mistakes through arrogant assumptions. The character grows as she learns to deal with complicated feelings.

This is particularly well done as she experiences a sweet, gentle romance. Millie Bobby Brown gives Enola Holmes tremendous depth. She's fearless when needed, but can still blush when a boy holds her hand. Enola Holmes does not give you all the answers. It's a solid tentpole film that establishes the primary characters and sets the framework for further mysteries. Enola Holmes is generally lighthearted, but dark and surprisingly violent at times. The action does get bloody, so be aware for younger viewers.'

(322) The Duffer Brothers said Millie was initially nervous about a girl (Sadie Sink) joining the cast of kids in Stranger Things 2. "Millie was very nervous about another girl coming: What is this going to be like? Now they're best friends. She's like, "Thank God for bringing in another girl, because I am so sick of these boys!""

(323) Millie doesn't seem to have much interest in video

games.

(324) Millie says she has always loved writing essays.

(325) In 2018, Millie voiced Darren Aronofsky's virtual reality experience Spheres: Songs of Spacetime.

(326) Millie made her modelling debut in Calvin Klein's By Appointment campaign in 2017.

(327) Millie won the Best TV Actress award at the 2017 Fangoria Chainsaw Awards.

(328) Stranger Things producer Shawn Levy said it was Millie's laser beam stare that convinced him she should play Eleven. "I've never forgotten it, because it was so intuitive. That this little person had such fierce power — that's what took me aback. That same day the Duffers and I knew she was the one."

(329) Not a single episode of Stranger Things had been written when Millie did her first audition. She didn't really know what the show was about. All she knew was that it was a science fiction show of some sort.

(330) It takes about two or three weeks to shoot an episode of Stranger Things. The special effects obviously take a lot longer than this to complete though.

(331) The Duffer Brothers said of Millie - "Millie's something special, alright, with a downright spooky preternatural talent. She inhabits every moment so intensely, with some alchemy of intelligence, preparation, and instinct. By the end of production, we found ourselves listening to Millie as if she were one of our most seasoned adult actors."

(332) David Harbour said it was quite difficult at first to shoot the confrontational scenes between Eleven and Hopper in Stranger Things 2 because Millie was so young. He found

though that Millie was more than capable of holding her own. "I had to work a lot harder while working with Millie, and I don't know exactly why. I think it's more complicated for me to yell at a young woman that way. It was very emotionally complex for me to play that. That was a really messed up day when we did that scene. I mean I was feeling all messed up about it. But I did want to treat the scene with the respect it deserves and I wanted to treat Millie with the respect she deserves as my female co-star, and really give her my all and my power, and she's able to give it right back. So that was a very complicated day."

(333) When they made season one of Stranger Things, the cast were not given all the scripts so they had no idea how it was going to end for most of the production.

(334) Millie says she is quite a big eater so has to work out a lot to burn off all the food.

(335) Millie has always wanted Hopper and Joyce to get together in Stranger Things because she would then get more scenes with Noah Schnapp (who plays Joyce's son in the show).

(336) Millie said that wearing a corset for Enola Holmes gave her an hourglass figure but it was only temporary and she soon lost it after shooting ended.

(337) Millie is a fan of The Conjuring horror movies.

(338) Millie had always been a Winona Ryder fan so she was very excited when she found out that Winona was also going to be in Stranger Things.

(339) Millie said that when she first watched Stranger Things 3 she watched a few episodes and then skipped to the finale to see how it would end. She then went back and watched it in the correct order. In mitigation you could say that she must have already had a good idea how it would end because she

was one of the main actors in the show!

(340) Millie has hazel eyes.

(341) Millie's first acting classes were in Orlando. She attended the classes on Saturdays.

(342) Millie's natural hair colour is dark brown.

(343) Millie dated the singer Jacob Sartorius but it did not last long.

(344) Millie is believed to have dated Joseph Robinson but this did not last long either. Joseph Robinson is the son of a famous English rugby player called Jason Robinson (who scored a winning try in the 2003 Rugby World Cup final). Joseph is also a rugby player.

(345) Millie is apparently known as Mills or the Millster to her friends and family.

(346) Millie loves blueberry ice cream.

(347) Millie is a fan of green juice.

(348) Millie is a big fan of the musical film Bugsy Malone.

(349) Millie won the Hero of the Year award at the 2017 NME Awards.

(350) Millie's first ever commercial was for Grand Floridian Spa.

(351) Millie said she has always been a fan of browsing in discount and bargain stores. She probably doesn't need to do that so much these days!

(352) Millie is a big fan of French fries. Being from England, Millie would call them chips.

(353) Millie thinks it's easier to act in roles you don't know much about beforehand because you have to rely on your instincts more.

(354) Millie is apparently a fan of Justin Bieber.

(355) Millie is a big fan of Leonardo DiCaprio.

(356) Millie said that even when she became world famous after the first season of Stranger Things she still had to do homework and chores when she was at home.

(357) Millie loves musicals.

(358) Millie said her partial deafness makes it difficult for her to sing but she always refused to stop trying because she loves singing.

(359) Millie is said to like Fidget spinners. A fidget spinner is a toy that consists of a ball bearing in the center of a multi-lobed (typically two or three) flat structure made from metal or plastic designed to spin along its axis with very little effort. Fidget spinners became trending toys in 2017, although similar devices had been invented as early as 1993. The toys are alleged to help with stress.

(360) Millie says she loves science.

(361) When Millie appeared on Gordon Ramsey's Hell's Kitchen as a ten year-old she ordered a toasted cheese sandwich.

(362) Millie uses lip oil and cleansing gel.

(363) Millie likes using peel off masks for her skin.

(364) Millie's natural hair is curly. You can see what her real hair looks like in Stranger Things 2 because Eleven has curls in

that season.

(365) Millie said the kids in the Stranger Things cast bonded by going to the Six Flags amusement park.

(366) Millie has two tortoises.

(367) Millie says she is inspired by the activist Greta Thunberg. Millie said she would happily play Greta in a film.

(368) Millie said she admires the character she plays in Stranger Things. "I have learned a lot from Eleven. Yes, she's powerful, but she is also a loyal friend and protector. Even though she's still learning how to use her voice, her resilience, loyalty and strength inspires me."

(369) Millie deleted her entire TikTok account in December 2020 and now has a private account.

(370) The Duffer Brothers said that when they started making Stranger Things they soon noticed that Millie could adjust her performance according to the position of the cameras. This was a very sophisticated and subtle thing for a child actor to have the ability to do.

(371) The Duffer Brothers originally planned for Mike and Eleven to be reunited at the Snowball dance in the finale of Stranger Things 2. The reunion actually took place though in the penultimate episode.

(372) Netflix floated the possibility of filming seasons two and three of Stranger Things back to back to mitigate the fact that the children (who were, you might plausibly argue, the trump card of the cast in season one) were growing up fast. The Duffer Brothers did not concur with this plan though. They were perfectly relaxed about the fact that the kids would be growing teenagers in new seasons.

(373) The relationship between Mike Wheeler and Eleven in

season one of Stranger Things is influenced by Tomas Alfredson's 2008 Swedish film Let the Right One In. Let the Right One In is also set in the early eighties and concerns two eleven year-old children - a boy named Oskar and a girl named Eli - who form a close bond. Oskar is bullied at school and Eli is a vampire. As with Eleven, Eli has to stay hidden and doesn't really understand the normal mundane everyday world. Like the character of Eleven, Eli also has special powers.

(374) Millie is a fan of the musical Annie.

(375) The scenes where Millie's character Eleven is in the lab's sensory deprivation water chamber in season one of Stranger Things are clearly very inspired by Anna Torv's character entering a sensory deprivation water tank for scientists in the Fox TV show Fringe.

(376) Eleven's ability to eat huge amounts of food in season one of Stranger Things might be a sly reference to the DC Comics superhero The Flash. The Flash has to eat a lot of food to replenish the energy expended by the use of his powers.

(377) Millie has described herself as a prankster.

(378) Millie thinks she is not a 'girly girl' and has a lot of tomboy qualities.

(379) Millie said eating Eggo waffles in the first season of Stranger Things was no picnic because the waffles they used were a bit stale.

(380) Millie said she once had an unfortunate experience at the UN building when the zip on her dress broke. She had to go and put on a different dress.

(381) Millie said she likes spicy food and anything with a bit of kick to it.

(382) In 2021, Millie made a generous donation to a food bank

in New Mexico while shooting Stranger Things 4.

(383) Full Circle Cinema wrote of the Enola Holmes movie - 'Millie Bobby Brown shines as Enola Holmes. She's quirky, but she manages to fit into the period piece incredibly well. The intermix of fourth-wall-breaking from Enola is of neat contrast to previous Sherlock Holmes incarnations. It serves as her thought processing, similar to Robert Downey Jr.'s time slow down in his Sherlock movies and Benedict Cumberbatch's writing in the air in the Sherlock series. It works well to differentiate her from the rest of the pack of Holmes, but also fits well within the storytelling.

The plot of the film feels simple. At the same time, it also does well as a mystery, and just encompasses a little bit of all genres. There's always a twist to keep you intrigued. The subtle romance between Tewksbury (Louis Partridge) and Enola is fun. But ultimately the highlight is Enola making it work in the period. In addition, it highlights the plight of women trying to start their own legacy. I enjoyed seeing the themes so played forward, bright and honest, just like Enola. Seeing Enola grow up with her mother builds a further emotional connection to both characters in Enola's search for her mother. Ultimately, she sees the truth to her mother's work in this coming of age story but allows herself to feel free to make her own choices. This includes interacting with Viscount Tewksbury, and Partridge accents Brown quite nicely.'

(384) When they shot the school classroom Demogorgon showdown in the season one Stranger Things finale, Millie and the boys had the giggles and kept laughing.

(385) In Stranger Things 3 there is a montage of Max and Eleven having fun at the mall. Sadie Sink and Millie were allowed to pick the activities that their characters took part in during this montage.

(386) The real name of Millie's character Eleven is Jane Ives.

(387) In the prequel novel Stranger Things - Suspicious Minds, we learn that Eleven was named Jane after the famed anthropologist and primatologist Jane Goodall.

(388) The costume designer on Stranger Things said Millie and the other kids never brought their high fashion attitudes onto the set and were always happy to wear what their characters were given. "They don't bring in their high fashion wants into the room because they know that's not what their characters are about. They're very professional. I've worked with a lot of very young actors in my career and these are some of the most talented, most fun, most professional actors I've ever worked with — at any age."

(389) Millie said that she and younger cast members in Stranger Things especially love night shoots.

(390) The Duffer Brothers said it was a great relief when they started shooting Stranger Things and saw the children were all excellent actors with good chemistry. As they pointed out, one bad performance from one of the children could have sunk the entire show!

(391) Millie said The Possession is one of the scariest films she has seen. The Possession is a 2012 horror film with Jeffrey Dean Morgan about a little girl who is possessed by a demon.

(392) The Duffer Brothers said they love Millie's telekinetic temper tantrums as Eleven in Stranger Things.

(393) Millie said that (perhaps unavoidably) most of her friends are from the film and television industry. She said she still has a few childhood friends from England though who knew her before she was famous.

(394) Of the kids in Stranger Things, Millie and Finn Wolfhard seem to have been the most successful in making the jump to movies.

(395) David Harbour and Winona Ryder have both expressed some concern at the intense fame which fell on Millie at a young age because of Stranger Things. The entertainment industry is sadly littered with child stars who fell off the rails when they got older. Happily though, Millie seems to be navigating fame fairly well and staying grounded.

(396) Millie says To Kill a Mockingbird is one of her favourite films.

(397) Stranger Things was partly inspired by what became known as The Montauk Project - a conspiracy theory that revolves around the (now decommissioned) Montauk Air Force Station located at the east end of the Long Island peninsula. The conspiracy theories surrounding the base include teleportation, time travel, and contact with aliens.

(398) One of Millie's co-stars in Enola Holmes was Superman star Henry Cavill. Henry played (a very buff) Sherlock Holmes in the film.

(399) Cyndi Lauper and Madonna songs were played on the set when Sadie Sink and Millie shot the mall montage for The Mall Rats episode in season three of Stranger Things.

(400) The montage of Eleven and Max shopping at the mall in Stranger Things 3 was inspired by a similar montage in the 1984 film Night of the Comet.

(401) Millie said it is always rather tricky trying to work out what to wear for a red carpet event. "It's always difficult to dress for a red carpet event because a lot of people have opinions and unfortunately you say you won't listen to it, but you actually kind of have to. For me, I sit there and think, I'm not going to listen to what they have to say, journalists or whoever wants to write badly about my inappropriate outfit."

(402) Millie has occasionally had criticism for dressing in a way that is too mature for age. She thinks this criticism is

unfair and a consequence of the fact that a lot of people still think of her as the little girl in season one of Stranger Things as if she is frozen in time. "Being a young girl, people watch you grow up, right?" said Millie. "And they've almost become invested in your growth and your journey, but they aren't ready to accept the fact that you're growing up."

(403) Mille has lent her name to the Pandora jewellery brand. "Pandora was one of the only brands I could afford," she said. "It was always so accessible with the pocket money I'd get, so it felt that it was a place where I belonged."

(404) Millie said she used to hate wearing heels but now she doesn't mind them so much.

(405) Millie said you have to have a thick skin to be an aspiring actor because you will unavoidably be rejected for most of the auditions you attend.

(406) Millie said she read the Enola Holmes books with her sister several years ago and had always wanted to play the character in a film.

(407) When she became an actor, Millie added 'Bobby' to her name as a way to avoid confusion with a performance artist named Millie Brown. These days though Millie's fame far outstrips that of the performance artist who shares her name!

(408) Millie said that when she was an aspiring child actor in England, her father couldn't take her to every audition in London because they couldn't always afford the petrol needed for the car journey.

(409) Millie said she loves taking a hot bath with essential oils.

(410) Stranger Things 2 broke a Twitter record by generating more than 3.7 million tweets about the show.

(411) Millie is a fan of Olivia Rodrigo.

(412) When Hopper visits Terry Ives in season one of Stranger Things, we see a picture of Alice in Jane's bedroom. this could be a sly in-joke because Millie played the young Alice in the TV show Once Upon A Time in Wonderland.

(413) Bradley's Big Buy grocery store in Palmetto, Ga (where Eleven steals the waffles in season one of Stranger Things) reported that their sales of Eggo waffles trebled when season three of Stranger Things came out.

(414) Millie said she had to cry a lot in her Stranger Things audition.

(415) Millie said that when she has a movie offer she usually asks her older sister to read the script to see if it's any good or would suit her.

(416) Millie said her worst beauty habit is not washing her makeup brushes often enough.

(417) Millie said that when she isn't acting she spends most of her time eating or writing.

(418) Millie said - "It can be difficult to be a young girl in the industry. Sometimes, people don't like to listen to what you have to say or dismiss you purely because you're young. But things are looking up, each day I am growing stronger and learning more."

(419) Eleven's pant suspenders in season three of Stranger Things appear to be a reference to Robin Williams in the sitcom Mork & Mindy.

(420) There is an Eggo card game based on Stranger Things.

(421) Millie said she would love to be in a romantic film some day.

(422) Millie is a fan of soda.

(423) Millie said she genuinely had no idea that Eleven was going to become such an iconic character.

(424) Millie thinks the character of Eleven became so popular because she is vulnerable and someone viewers naturally want to help.

(425) Eleven's punk makeover in Stranger Things 2 makes her look like Ally Sheedy in The Breakfast Club - although this might be a coincidence. The Breakfast Club is a 1985 teen drama by John Hughes. John Hughes was one of the many influences on Stranger Things.

(426) Helena Bonham-Carter, who played Millie's mother in Enola Holmes, described Millie as a "powerhouse" actor.

(427) Millie said that, between production, she sometimes goes weeks and months without seeing her Stranger Things co-stars but they instantly slide back into their friendships when they meet up again.

(428) Millie said The Bathtub is her favourite season one episode of Stranger Things. "The reason I picked the episode is because it starts off like this and climaxes and then slowly goes down again, and then neutralises itself. It was a big, big transition, kind of like a journey for Eleven. That's the reason I chose it."

(429) Eggo sales went up by 15% after Stranger Things 2 came out.

(430) Millie has multiple ear piercings.

(431) Millie said that fashion and music are her big passions outside of acting.

(432) Millie said she likes avocado and tomato in her salad.

(433) Millie said that (unlike other actors) she actually loves learning lines so it came as something of a surprise when got the first season one scripts for Stranger Things and saw that her character Eleven barely speaks!

(434) Stranger Things casting director Carmen Cuba said it is not easy putting children through auditions because most of them are unavoidably going to be rejected. "I've had young actors leave auditions and later be told that they were very upset. Being a mom I am extra sensitive to kids--it's a very hard thing to do, to go into a room and really be tested on hard material--but other people in the room aren't always in tune with the fact that these kids are really putting it on the line for them and that it's hard emotionally. But it's a business, unfortunately, and kid actors are a tricky thing on lots of levels."

(435) Netflix say that Stranger Things is so popular they even had a viewer in Antarctica.

(436) Finn Wolfhard said of Millie - "If you put something on her shoulders, something big or a big scene, she'll figure it out. She can handle pressure very well."

(437) Millie said it was very exciting when she was asked to test for Stranger Things because she wasn't being offered many auditions at the time.

(438) Millie said that the best decompression chamber for fame is simply to concentrate on work.

(439) Millie said she doesn't watch that many films because she rarely has the patience to sit through them.

(440) Millie said she did Amy Winehouse impressions at a young age.

(441) Inverse.Com wrote - 'The star of Enola Holmes is Millie

Bobby Brown, and she inhabits the role completely. If you're expecting the socially awkward superhero tween from Stranger Things, you've got another thing coming. Enola is funny with a dry wit, trading barbs with allies and villains alike — her under-explored dynamic with Cavill is particularly interesting. She's also got some serious fight moves (or a very convincing stunt double), and when she cracks each clue left by her mom without breaking a sweat, you really believe she's a Sherlock-level genius.'

(442) Millie said shooting Godzilla: King of the Monsters was tough because she had to do a lot of running.

(443) Millie said the My Moon Dangle Charm is her favourite thing in the Pandora collection.

(444) Millie said she enjoyed wearing all the Victorian clothes in Enola Holmes - aside from the corset.

(445) Millie said her favourite Liverpool player was always Philippe Coutinho. She must have been disappointed though because they sold him to Barcelona in the end.

(446) Millie says she always sleeps with a glass of water by her bed.

(447) The radio Hopper and Eleven keep in contact on in Stranger Things 2 is tuned to broadcast channel 11.

(448) The fact that Eleven was going to come back in Stranger Things 2 was such a big secret that Millie wasn't even allowed to tell her family at first!

(449) Millie said she had so few lines in season one of Stranger Things that whenever she was given something to say it felt like a Christmas present.

(450) Millie said it was quite intense working with Dacre Montgomery (who plays Billy Hargrove) in Stranger Things 3

because he was a method actor and got into a sullen mood for his scenes.

(451) Matt Duffer, one of the co-creators of Stranger Things, said of Millie - "We have yet to give her something that she's unable to do. I can throw this girl an incredible fastball, she's going to hit it. It's like a singer who can hit any note. Her range is just absolutely incredible. I have yet to see any limits to it."

(452) Millie said she has a love hate relationship with crop tops.

(453) Millie said the other kids in the Stranger Things cast helped her get her American accent right when she played Eleven.

(454) IT'SUGAR released a I Dump Your Ass Stranger Things chocolate bar with Eleven and Mike on the wrapper.

(455) In season three of Stranger Things, Mike and Eleven have some M&Ms and you see a few red ones. This is a mistake because there were no red M&Ms in 1985 thanks to a health scare about red food dye.

(456) Eleven in the improvised sensory deprivation kiddie pool in season one of Stranger Things evokes the pre-cogs using a bathtub to tune in on future events in Steven Spielberg's film Minority Report.

(457) Millie said of David Harbour (who plays Eleven's dad in Stranger Things) - "David is one of my favorite people. He's very talented. I learn something new from him every day, so he deserves every award on the planet. He's someone I look up to. I am in awe of what he can do as an actor."

(458) Millie said she is a bit wary of wearing anything red because that's quite a mature fashion colour.

(459) Millie said Wonderwall by Oasis was one of the first

songs she sang as a child.

(460) Millie said when she worked on Modern Family she was very envious of the cast members who were regulars. "On Modern Family I was just envious of the other kids who were regulars on the show. I was just like a guest star and I just really wanted to be a regular you know with a trailer. I had a tiny little tent I had to change in."

(461) Millie said she usually has to get up at 6am when she's shooting Stranger Things.

(462) Millie said she wasn't happy at first when Sadie Sink joined the gang of children in season two of Stranger Things 2 but she soon changed her mind. "I was stressing out to be honest with you. I was the only girl. There's a ton of boys and they're a gang and you can't ever break that. And Sadie came in the first day and immediately I loved her. She is the sweetest person ever. The first night we met and I had tickets to Adele and I brought her with me. Then I took her to see Sia. And we had our first sleepover and we are best friends."

(463) Millie said it is still surreal to think of herself as a famous person.

(464) Millie says she always misses playing Eleven during breaks between production on Stranger Things.

(465) When Nancy stops off at the store in Stranger Things 3 to find some bandages for Eleven's wound, the store is Bradley's Big Buy - the same place where Eleven stole the waffles in season one.

(466) Costume designer Amy Parris said that Eleven's romper dress in season three was a vintage dress they found from a costume house in Los Angeles called Western Costume. The good thing about the dress was that it fit Millie Bobby Brown perfectly and had never been worn before.

(467) When it comes to fans and boundaries, Millie said -

"Boundaries and privacy are one of the things that I think is very important, but fans should understand that if [actors] are out at dinner and they feel they want to spend time with their family. Most of my fans have been wonderfully understanding, so it would be very easy for me to tell a fan, 'Hey, can you give me two seconds to finish my meal and I'll be right over.'

There's the odd person that will say things, but not everyone is going to like the person you are. My co-stars have experienced that a lot. I've been ever so lucky to go through it sometimes, but most of all I accept the fact that maybe [fans] just didn't understand correctly. It's weird because nobody understands [celebrity] except if you've been through it. I try to inform fans that I'm a person and I'm going through something extremely overwhelming sometimes. I'm a very anxious person, I will never hide that from people, but I think as long as you inform them and start making them understand, then they'll be fine."

(468) The Duffers have not specifically cited it as an influence, but season one of Stranger Things has the same premise as a Richard Matheson penned Twilight Zone episode called Little Girl Lost. Matheson's story is about a scientist who must rescue his daughter after she becomes trapped in an alternate dimension thanks to a portal in her bedroom.

(469) When Eleven is watching television alone in the cabin in Stranger Things 2 she imitates Susan Lucci while watching All My Children.

(470) A 2016 poll in Time Out named Hawkins as the fictional place where people would most like to go on vacation. King's Landing and Hogwarts were second and third.

(471) Millie is a big cat lover.

(472) Waitresses at the Stranger Things 2 premiere were dressed in special Eggo yellow uniforms.

(473) One of the influences on the character of Eleven was the Stephen King novel Carrie (which also became a film). The title character Carrie is a troubled girl with powerful telekinetic abilities.

(474) Millie says she has a low boredom threshold and finds it difficult to sit still.

(475) If you look very closely you can see that Eleven has a picture of Mike in his Ghostbusters costume on her bedside table in Stranger Things 3.

(476) Stranger Things costume designer Amy Parris said of dressing Millie in season three - "How do you dress the girl who's been secluded in a cabin for a year? She'd likely want to wear colorful patterns and prints. We landed on the stuff that felt the brightest and boldest. Millie was extremely helpful and I relied on her opinion a lot."

(477) Regarding former child stars who have gone off the rails, Millie said - "I hear this almost every day. People come up to me and say, Make time to be a kid. Make sure you stay humble. Make sure you're grounded. Make sure you're always playing with your friends. And I'm like, 'Listen, I'm pretty good so far. And you can't compare me to other actors who might have just made a wrong turn on their path. I am my own individual self and mistakes are part of life."

(478) Eleven's clothes and curly hair in season two of Stranger Things make her look a lot like Jenny Matrix in the 1985 action film Commando.

(479) Charlie Heaton, who plays Jonathan Byers in Stranger Things, is also from England like Millie.

(480) David Harbour said he feels very protective of Millie because he knew her when she was very young and not yet famous.

(481) Millie said of social media -

"We (young people) were born into social media. So that's all I've ever known, is social media. That's all us kids have ever known. But we deal with social media smarter than some people that hadn't had it. We know that social media is an incredible place to spread a message — and a really bad place to bully, access negative hate, violence, and exploitation.

I guess one thing that they should remember about social media is that we should make it into a really positive place where everyone feels welcomed and everyone feels like they're part of a bit of a community. We're slowly getting there, I think. Social media will become a better place in the future if we all work hard at it."

(482) Millie is a fan of Teen Beach Movie. This is a 2013 Disney channel film. She knows the songs by heart.

(483) Millie said she would like to have a music career one day.

(484) Mike tries to contact Eleven at 7:40 p.m in Stranger Things 2. 7 + 4 = 11.

(485) Joe Keery (who plays Steve Harrington) said the Stranger Things kids threw him out of their chat group for being too old!

(486) Millie said she doesn't like pizza. She says people find this odd because most people love pizza.

(487) A survey in 2017 found 31% of young adults had watched all the episodes of Stranger Things.

(488) Eleven falling into Mike's arms after Eleven battles Billy in The Sauna Test episode of Stranger Things 3 was not in the script but something Millie did on instinct. The director

Shawn Levy liked this improvisation and kept it in the episode.

(489) No one seems to call Eleven by her real name Jane in Stranger Things. She's always El or Eleven to her friends!

(490) Millie said that on Enola Holmes her performance was always better when she was in costume. When she rehearsed her lines in casual modern clothes she couldn't get into the character.

(491) Millie said of the other kids in the Stranger Things cast - "We kids are like siblings. There's no other way really to describe it. We're not best friends. We're like brothers and sisters. We've never even talked about dating to each other. That isn't even part of this. It's genuine friendship. And we experience everything together."

(492) At the end of season two of Stranger Things, Eleven blanks Max when they are first introduced. Sadie Sink said - "Eleven hasn't met many girls her own age before, so when she saw Max she immediately saw her as a threat."

(493) The number of the bus Eleven rides to find Kali/Eight in Stranger Things 2 is 422. 4 + 2 + 2 = 8.

(494) The Duffers decided to take Eleven's powers away at the end of Stranger Things 3 to add more tension. They were mindful of the fact that Eleven's powers had saved everyone in the previous two finales and didn't want the end of each season to be exactly the same.

(495) The costume designers on Stranger Things researched eighties fashions in vintage issues of Tiger Beat and Cosmopolitan magazines.

(496) Eleven's reaction to finally seeing Mike again in the penultimate episode of Stranger Things 2 was a remarkable piece of acting by Millie because Finn Wolfhard wasn't on the set and she had to pretend he was there and react to nothing.

(497) In their first review of Stranger Things back in 2016, Variety wrote - 'All that said, Stranger Thing greatest accomplishment may be in the casting of its younger characters. Millie Brown plays a key figure in the series, and her storyline would likely be ruined if it were discussed in any depth. All you really need to know is that she is note-perfect in her role, which requires her to be both an enigmatic object of scrutiny and a regular kid who is put in an array of confusing and difficult situations. She pulls off everything that is asked of her and more with exceptional facility and subtlety.'

(498) Millie has met Ariana Grande and Taylor Swift.

(499) Millie said she is partial to a caramel frappuccino.

(500) In an interview for the third season of Stranger Things, the producer Shawn Levy said it was important in Stranger Things to adapt to the fact that the younger cast members are growing up fast. "The key for us as producers and directors is don't pretend they're not changing. Adjust the story to meet the actors where they are. So hopefully in season three, we've told stories that reflect the ages they're at and the developmental changes physically, emotionally that our actors are going through. You see those incorporated on screen."

(501) Millie said she loves cheese.

(502) In their review of Stranger Things when it came out in 2016, the Los Angeles Times wrote - 'Ryder is great, Harbour grows on you, but Stranger Things belongs to the kids, especially the five young ones. Millie Bobby Brown is the most obvious marvel. With their pastiche of genres, the Duffer brothers manage to skirt the hideous abuse El has endured (though the tattoo, shaved head and initial starvation dangerously evoke real horror), but El is taut with the tension between real power and inflicted powerlessness. If certain scenes dwell too long on her silence or enormous eyes, that is not Brown's fault. With few words, she manages to evoke a

cacophony of emotion, from terror to tender young love.'

(503) Millie has attended quite a few fan conventions to talk about Stranger Things.

(504) There has been a lot of speculation lately that Marvel want Millie to be in one of their movies but at the time of writing this hasn't happened. "Everybody thinks I'm going to be in a Marvel movie," said Millie. "Not that I know of. My family and I have no idea. So I just want to let everyone know that I'm not as of right now."

(505) The fame of Stranger Things is such that it was the subject of a jovial Sesame Street parody in 2017.

(506) David Harbour said of Millie -

"My hope with Millie has and is always that she will be an artist, that when I am in the nursing home, she will bring me her Oscars. But, I feel like the pitfalls are very deep in terms of this generation; this fame, this Instagram generation of constantly wanting to get likes. I never really grew up with that and the fact that there is somebody with eleven million followers or something like, that's thinking about their persona to the world at thirteen or fourteen years of age is terrifying to me.

I know she has tremendous potential and my hope is that she can remain grounded and protected as much as possible. I'm protective of her. I want her to grow up to become Meryl Steep. I don't want her in rehab at 20, or whatever, because she's a child star. I know she's super talented, but they all were talented and there is this trajectory of tension and spotlight placed on a young, developing person, which, to me, is terrifying, seen through parental eyes."

(507) Most of the networks who rejected Stranger Things wanted the show to lose the kids and focus on Hopper as the central character. Anyone who thought Stranger Things would

be improved by removing all the children clearly didn't really understand what the Duffers were doing at all!

(508) An early plan for Stranger Things was that the second season would have a time jump and would take place in 1990 when the kids are now young adults and must reunite to fight the strange forces threatening their village again. This was patently inspired by Stephen King's IT and an element in the pitch that never happened in the end.

The vague notion of setting a second season of the show in 1990 ten years later (the original plan was for Stranger Things to begin in 1980) quickly became obsolete when Stranger Things began shooting and the Duffers saw how good the child actors were. The notion of having a second season of Strangers Things with the likes of Millie and Gaten Matarazzo replaced by older actors was unthinkable.

(509) Millie is a fan of plaid when it comes to fashion.

(510) Millie has lilac eyeshadow as Eleven at the Snow Ball dance in the Stranger Things 2 finale.

(511) Millie said she likes to play Badmington in the garden with her sister.

(512) The void of nothingness that represents Eleven's mindscape in Stranger Things was influenced by Under the Skin. Under the Skin is 2013 film with Scarlett Johansson as an alien who preys on victims in a void of nothing with a puddled liquid floor.

(513) Millie said that home-schooling worked well for her and she never had any desire to go back to a real school.

(514) Millie is sometimes compared to Emma Watson in that both are British and became famous as child actors. Millie met Emma Watson at the MTV awards a few years back.

(515) Millie is friends with rap superstar Drake.

(516) Just before Stranger Things came along, a casting agent told Millie she had become too mature for child roles and had probably missed the window to become a famous child actress. He was obviously wrong about this.

(517) Despite being an actor, Millie has not lived in Hollywood yet because her family don't think it's a good place for her to stay grounded.

(518) Millie is a fan of the TV show Friday Night Lights.

(519) Millie is a big fan of dolphins.

(520) Millie said her parents helped her come up with the body language she used to play Eleven.

(521) In the video game Silent Hill: Homecoming there is a girl named Elle with super powers who has lived in a hospital. This doesn't seem like a coincidence because the Duffer Brothers are big Silent Hill fans.

(522) Eleven trying to move the train in The Lost Sister is patently a homage to Luke Skywalker trying to raise his X-Wing from the swamp in The Empire Strikes Back.

(523) When it comes to food, Millie said you can't beat a good sandwich.

(524) Stranger Things costume designer Amy Parris said that they have to have multiples of the kids outfits for stunt doubles and stand-ins to use. This makes the task of sourcing period clothes even more complex.

(525) Millie is a fan of Sriracha. Sriracha is a chilli sauce made from peppers.

(526) The Triple-Decker Eggo Extravaganza (a modest 8,000

calories) that Hopper makes for Eleven in Stranger Things 2 consists of waffles, whipped cream, Reese's Pieces, Hershey's Kisses, and jelly beans.

(527) Starbucks introduced a Stranger Things Eleven Frappuccino on one of their secret menus. It had a caramel and waffle theme.

(528) According to a study, females make up 57% of the Stranger Things audience.

(529) Millie basically had to mimic stars of the silent era in season one of Stranger Things.

(530) The sequence that gave the designers and special effects team on Stranger Things the most headaches was the school classroom showdown between Eleven and the Demogorgon in the season one finale. The lighting and cloud of dust that envelops Eleven and the monster was exceptionally difficult to get right.

(531) Millie wears reading glasses in real life.

(532) In their review of Stranger Things when it came out in 2016, Vulture wrote - 'The real revelation is Millie Bobby Brown. As the enigmatic, often silent Eleven, a girl with telekinetic powers and the closely shaven haircut of a cancer patient undergoing chemo, Brown conveys a range of emotions — fear, confusion, raw fury — using only her eyes and a face that itself seems like a portal into some parallel universe. In such a Spielbergian project, the Duffer brothers undoubtedly wanted their Eleven to have a genuine Spielberg face. Brown's definitely got one; you watch her and you're reminded of Henry Thomas in E.T. and Samantha Morton in Minority Report all at once. When she gets to share the screen with Ryder, who was roughly the same age as Brown when she landed her first role in the movie Lucas, it's a lovely, circle-of-life moment.'

(533) Millie said she likes television because the shooting pace is faster than a movie.

(534) Millie also said though that the advantage with acting in movies is that you have more time to do a take or a scene.

(535) Millie is a fan of the singer Jon Bellion.

(536) Millie is a fan of the TV show Queer Eye.

(537) Millie's kiss from Finn Wolfhard at the end of the first season of Stranger Things was her first ever kiss from anyone both onscreen or off.

(538) Millie is a fan of Blake Lively.

(539) When the first season of Stranger Things came out, The Guardian's reviewer wrote -

'All the child actors – especially Millie Bobby Brown as the forlorn ex-lab rat Eleven – are so good that they confirm my theory that Area 51 has nothing to do with aliens, but is the place where Hollywood farms its juvenile leads. Just as Eleven was apparently plucked from her mentally-unstable mother's womb by Brenner's team of sinister scientists 12 years ago, so children all over America are whisked off the minute they show the slightest ability to hit a mark to the Dakota Fanning School of Weirdly Automated Instinct (formerly the Shirley Temple Charm School) and drilled in the art of sitcom, drama and film under a regime that would make even Soviet gymnasts balk.'

(540) In the Portuguese language version of Stranger Things, Eggo waffles are called panqueques. Panqueques means pancakes.

(541) Millie thinks Stranger Things is popular because the outcasts and outsiders are the heroes in the show.

(542) Millie said she would like to work with Steven Spielberg one day.

(543) Millie said she was a fan of The Vampire Diaries. The Vampire Diaries is an American supernatural teen drama television series that ended in 2017.

(544) Millie said that although she loves fashion she doesn't especially enjoy going shopping.

(545) Millie said that Zendaya is one of her fashion inspirations.

(546) Millie said that, as a producer on the movie, she was involved in the casting for Enola Holmes.

(547) Millie said of working with Helena Bonham Carter on Enola Holmes - "Helena Bonham Carter is obviously a legend, so I watched her and studied her. I was impressed by every take. She's so versatile and I aspire to be like that. I'm following in the footsteps of these incredible women that have had amazing careers and are still going, and I was just very lucky to be in her presence for nine-and-a-half hours a day."

(548) Millie said she is a fan of baking. She finds it very relaxing.

(549) Millie likes gardening.

(550) Millie wore upside down eye shadow at the 2017 San Diego Comic-Con.

(551) The broken kneecap Millie was recovering from at the start of production on Stranger Things 3 was sustained when she slipped by the side of a swimming pool.

(552) Millie said that she is not bothered by how many social media followers she has. "I don't care so much about the numbers, I care more about the base of my fans, that is those

who follow me from the beginning of Stranger Things, they are lovely people."

(553) Millie said the late Audrey Hepburn is one of her great heroes.

(554) Millie said she hopes Eleven gets her powers back in Stranger Things 4. Eleven lost her powers at the end of season three.

(555) Millie said it scares her to think of Stranger Things ending one day. "I don't even want to talk about it, it gets me too upset."

(556) Of her character in Stranger Things, Millie said - "I don't call her Jane, she will never be Jane to me. She is Eleven or El to me."

(557) Millie said the scenes with Eleven and Matthew Modine's Dr Brenner in the first season of Stranger Things were the most emotionally draining she has ever done.

(558) Millie said that when she broke her kneecap prior to Stranger Things 3 she got a giant get well card and lots of gifts from the cast and crew.

(559) Millie is a fan of Bruno Mars.

(560) Millie's father serves as her manager.

(561) Millie has endorsed Penshoppe. Penshoppe is a casual wear retail brand based in the Philippines.

(562) Millie loves the scent of cucumber.

(563) Millie's makeup range is named after her late great-grandmother Florence.

(564) Millie has endorsed Samsung.

(565) Millie designed some of her own glasses with Vogue eyewear.

(566) Millie has some fish.

(567) Millie said she spends a lot of time in the garden trying to save insects.

(568) On shaving her hair to play Eleven in Stranger Things, Millie said - "It's just hair; it doesn't define me as a girl."

(569) Millie said she is inspired by Malala Yousafzai. Malala Yousafzai is a Pakistani activist for female education and the youngest Nobel Prize laureate.

(570) Millie won Best Sci-Fi/Fantasy TV Actress at the 2018 Teen Choice Awards.

(571) Millie said she auditioned for the musical Matilda when she was a little kid.

(572) Millie's father said she was always loud and a big personality as a child.

(573) After the end of production on season one of Stranger Things, Millie went back to England and started to think about what her next job might be. She had no idea that Stranger Things would become a global phenomenon and profoundly change her life.

(574) Millie said it was a great thrill to meet Justin Timberlake in 2018.

(575) Millie is friends with Paris Jackson. Paris is the daughter of the later Michael Jackson.

(576) Millie is a fan of Rihanna.

(577) The Playlist wrote of Enola Holmes - 'Brown easily carries the film, has tremendous chemistry with everyone, and radiates appealing charisma— it's no wonder Netflix hasn't let her stray very far from their algorithm (she's far more interesting here than "Stranger Things" ever allowed her to be). Cavill is yet another winning surprise. Often not quite convincing in his own acting skin, especially when playing an American, the British actor demonstrates just how effortless he is when playing cool, collected debonair gentlemen (truly, he and Brown, could make a career and mint solely starring in English period films if they chose, they are so perfect for it). Likewise, Claflin is often uncomfortably shoehorned into leading man roles, but free to be the smug, haughty, intolerant Mycroft, he is an absolute joy to watch.'

(578) Millie thinks that the key to playing Eleven is not to overthink the character and play it purely through instinct. "Eleven is part of me and always will be. I don't even know my lines for today's scene ... and that's what makes it so instinctual."

(579) Millie is a fan of Topshop.

(580) Mille said the kids often play card games on the set of Stranger Things.

(581) Millie said she would love to do a show on Broadway one day.

(582) Millie says that when she visits Winona Ryder's trailer on Stranger Things they usually have cheese and crackers.

(583) Maddie Ziegler said of Millie - "She can rock any style. She is not afraid to wear clothes that some kids would be afraid to wear and she also has kind of the same style as me — kind of tomboyish. She loves jeans and t-shirts like I do, so I would say that she is a good representation of what I would be inspired by. I think girls shouldn't be afraid to wear what they want to wear, even if they think they're going to be judged."

(584) When Millie's family first visited Los Angeles with her, Millie was offered representation by nearly every acting agent who met with her.

(585) Millie said she has always liked purple as a colour.

(586) Millie has been all over the world to talk about Stranger Things. She has been to places like Australia and Argentina.

(587) When she was thirteen, Millie said she would like to go to college at the age of eighteen. Her acting career seems to have made this unlikely though.

(588) Millie is a fan of milkshakes. She especially likes a chocolate brownie shake.

(589) Millie enjoys baking chocolate chip cookies in particular. Being from England she would call them biscuits.

(590) Millie is a big fan of Zac Efron.

(591) Stranger Things producer Shawn Levy said that casting child actors is quite different from casting adult actors. "I'm looking for not only talent, but that special synchronicity between the actor and the character. So, with the kids on our show, we definitely talk with them more before and after their reading than we do with most adults auditioning. With an adult actor, you're betting so much on the reading. With a kid actor, you're betting just as much on their innate quality in real life in the room.

I can tell you for a fact we saw 1,000 kids [for] Stranger Things, and many, many talented kids didn't get the part. I always tell my actor friends, you can nail an audition and you can be incredibly talented, and sometimes you still won't get the part if it's not in sync with the filmmakers' vision of that character and their feeling—or lack of feeling)—that that person is in the room with them. So much of it comes down to that stuff beyond an actor's control. That's important to remember so you don't beat yourself up for the wrong reasons."

(592) Millie said she doesn't really dress up much for Halloween because she dresses up all the time for movie and television roles and photo shoots.

(593) Eleven has the baby mask she wore while with Kali's gang in The Lost Sister hanging on her bedroom wall in Stranger Things 3.

(594) Stranger Things costume designer Amy Parris said that Eleven's romper dress in Stranger Things 3 is "a vintage piece we found from a costume house in Los Angeles called Western Costume. When I was first prepping in L.A., my team and I were pulling racks of clothes to send to Atlanta, where the season filmed. The romper immediately jumped out at me and I knew it was going to be a memorable item — it's so '80s. It fit Millie like a glove. She threw it on and felt so great in it. We had pulled some other heightened fashion pieces for the mall montage scene, but when we showed this one to the Duffer Brothers, there was no question.

It was Millie's favorite, too. I don't think it had ever been worn; it was totally brand-new. The fabric was in perfect condition, so it must not have been in Western Costume for long. Because I would imagine anybody pulling for an '80s show would have snatched it up, too. I was there at the right time!"

(595) In their review of Enola Holmes, Variety wrote - 'Millie Bobby Brown (who could pass for Sherlock star Benedict Cumberbatch's sister) brings some of the awkwardness we traditionally associate with the iconic detective to her role: Enola was never indoctrinated by her mother in the ways of polite society, and as such, she's meant to represent female intellect in its natural, unrepressed state. Her performance may be incongruous with the era, but that's hardly a bad thing.

Brown's acting style recalls the effusive spontaneity Keira Knightley brought to "Pride and Prejudice," shattering the straitlaced propriety of so many Jane Austen adaptations before it.
'

(596) There are some Sweet Valley High books in Eleven's bedroom in Stranger Things 3.

(597) The scenes where Eleven is in a black void of nothing in season one of Stranger Things were very inexpensive and easy to design. "It's just an inch of water on the ground, said Ross Duffer, "and then we just hung up black curtains, and suddenly we're in Eleven's head. It's cool how you can achieve something that we think is such a big idea so simply."

(598) Stranger Things extras casting director Heather Taylor said she was confident the show would be a hit because the children were so talented. "The moment I met the creators and the cast I knew it was going to be giant success. These kids have the most incredible personalities and are so unique- they also embody the traits of their characters, and are fantastic actors- that's a trifecta right there. There are no current shows out there that have a main cast of almost all kids, unless you're watching Disney or Nickelodeon (which is targeted for one specific age group). This show felt relatable to every age, from kids to adults. I would get totally lost from the outside world when I would read the scripts, not to mention how much everyone loves the 80s (including myself), how could this not be a hit!"

(599) Millie said that before she became famous she was happy to just lounge around in a tracksuit.

(600) During promotion for Stranger Things 3, director/producer Shawn Levy seemed to concede that The Lost Sister episode in Stranger Things 2 (which gave a solo spotlight to Eleven and took the action away from Hawkins to Chicago) was an experiment that didn't quite work. "As far as the dos and don'ts, there's nothing codified and written down,

but I would say the only big, memorable lesson we've learned was with episode seven of Season 2 when we get away from our core. When we leave Hawkins, and more critically when we leave our characters for an extended time, we tend to lose our anchor into the things that make us Stranger Things. So while episode seven, Eleven in Chicago, was an idea that was really fascinating on paper, I think we and our fans felt, that while it was a noble exploration, it got away from our DNA in a way that we won't be so quick to do again. We learned some valuable lessons there, but like most lessons in life, it has to be learned by trying rather than by being told."

(601) Millie thinks that Enola Holmes was an important project for her because it finally banished any fear she might be forever typecast as the troubled supernatural girl.

(602) Becky Ives mentions Stephen King in season one of Stranger Things. The subtext is that Eleven's backstory is similar to the little girl in Stephen King's Firestarter.

(603) The TV dinner Hopper and Eleven sit down to at the end of the first episode of Stranger Things 2 is sliced turkey with gravy, peas and mashed potatoes.

(604) Stranger Things designer Lachlan Milne said the sequences of Eleven's mindscape in season three had no green screen work. "It's pretty much all in-camera. It's all on a sound stage. There's a bit of VFX clean-up work, but we try and do most of that in-camera. The biggest thing is to try and keep light off it, because it's easy enough to pull the blacks into the grays. You have to pull the blacks down, but it affects the overall contrast of the scene. If there happens to be a little bit of light that bleeds through on the background, it turns what should be black into a mild gray. The real key is to keep as much light off the background as you can, and make sure that you fill out your foreground with enough detail so that when you actually put more contrast in the final image, you don't lose the detail or your foreground to contrasting."

(605) Millie says she always watches reality television with her mother when she's at home.

(606) Millie unsuccessfully auditioned for the musical Annie when she was a kid. Her Stranger Things co-star Sadie Sink was more successful and played Annie on the stage.

(607) Millie said that David Harbour drives her mad because he is always threatening to give away Stranger Things spoilers!

(608) Millie said that drinking plenty of water is part of her health regime.

(609) Millie said - "I don't care what I look like; it's how people think of me. I do care how people think of me. I want people to say, 'Oh, she's nice,' rather than, 'Oh, she's so pretty.'"

(610) Millie has won a couple of Kids' Choice Awards in the category of Favorite TV Actress for her role in Stranger Things.

(611) Millie said - "At the end of the day, I just do my job. I love my art. But I genuinely want to change the world. I'm very generous, and I really want people to see that I am – that's really it."

(612) Stranger things costume designer Amy Parris said of Eleven's pain splatter shirt with high-waisted jeans and suspenders outfit in Stranger Things 3 - "This outfit came about from a bit of necessity and the amount of time needed to execute it. Since Millie is a child actor who could only have limited work hours, we often needed multiples of her outfits to accommodate the longer filming time. I was lucky that the pants came in triples — we had three vintage DoorDash jeans that we found at Eastern Costume in Los Angeles. So we knew we could base the outfit off the jeans, which had the suspenders already built in.

The shirt was made from fabric we printed and remade, and

it's based on an '80s design. It actually has a fishtail tie, but we ended up tucking it in and not showing it — in the moment, the outfit was best without it. The fabric is inspired by a vintage splatter-print shirt. We digitized the print, and then printed the fabric. We had to make multiples so the pattern pieces matched perfectly for each one, which took a pretty long time."

(613) Millie earned a fortune on Enola Holmes because she also got an extra fee for being the producer. It was alleged that Millie got an extra $500,000 for being one of the producers.

(614) Millie said the worst thing about having a shaved head (to play Eleven in season one of Stranger Things) was going out in the rain.

(615) When it comes to eighties toys, Millie said she would rather have a Rubik's Cube than a Game Boy. She says that video games give her a headache.

(616) Millie said that Enola Holmes was a tough shoot because she had to do fight scenes and stunts.

(617) Millie has been known to showcase her love for grilled cheese sandwiches on Instagram.

(618) "I don't think I've changed," said Millie in 2018. "I'm not thinking, Oh, I know everything now. I still get nervous. I still get anxious."

(619) Stranger Things costume designer Amy Parris said of Eleven's yellow and black button-up, paired with crisscross suspenders and jeans costume in season three - "This look goes back to some images we found in Seventeen from 1984 and 1985. A lot of the fashion spreads had girls playing around with strong accessories, belts and suspenders — it was a big few years for accessories. A few girls in the magazine had the crisscross-suspender look, and I felt it was such a strong look that I knew I had to have Millie wear it for her ending scenes.

With each fitting for this final look, we'd always try the crisscross suspenders. At first we did it with a tank top, but it felt a little too revealing. It needed to be with something that blended in, so we found that it balanced well with a patterned shirt. We wanted to go bolder in our patterns, which we did, from splatter to yellow and black.

We made those pants from scratch, and the shirt is also from fabric we printed and made. Those jeans were a wonder. It had this incredible double waistband, and at the bottom it tapers to an intricate, patterned stitching detail. You never see those details on TV, so when we were creating the pants I was like, Nobody is going to notice the bottom of these pants, but they're so cool, damn it! And luckily, as I'm reading the script one day, Eleven's leg is injured, and we had to cut her pants open for the scene. So you can see it! The amount of work put into those pants was insane. It was a 19-piece pattern, which is kind of unheard of for pants. I was driving our tailors nuts, but I was like, "You know what? We have to go big for this last outfit."

You get to see her vintage Reebok sneakers too. They were bought in Atlanta at a vintage market. Those are very hard to find, and we knew we would need multiples, so we approached Levi's and asked if they'd help us with creating a few more pairs. They were able to re-create half of it — putting green leather on the outside, but not on the inside, so we painted the inside green to match the original shoes. So we had one vintage pair, and then a few molds that we mixed around for Millie and her stunt doubles."

(620) Millie says she tries to impersonate Maddie Ziegler but her dancing isn't great so the impression is a bit hit or miss.

(621) The beach scenes in Stranger Things 3 were shot in Malibu. Some of the first unofficial set photographs to emerge in the press were of Millie on a beach as Eleven. Shooting on a beach obviously made privacy more difficult than shooting on a set in Atlanta.

(622) Millie says her favourite dessert is chocolate mousse.

(623) Millie is a fan of the musical Chicago.

(624) Millie says she likes the 1980s because it seemed like a time when children had more freedom.

(625) Meghan Trainor and the pop group Little Mix attended Millie's sixteenth birthday party.

(626) Millie owns a Mini Cooper car.

(627) Millie says she usually has ginger shots in her fridge. Ginger shots are compact drinks made from juiced or grated ginger root.

(628) Celebrity Net Worth reported that the sequel to Enola Holmes will net Millie $7.5 million.

(629) Millie's acceptance speech when she won two MTV awards in 2017 was as follows - "Whoa. Oh, my goodness. This is extremely heavy. This is special to me. All right, first I want to thank everyone who voted and especially MTV. I would like to thank Netflix, Ian Patterson, Stan Cullen, thank the crew for being my second family. Guys, I love you. And I want to thank — I want to thank my family. I love you guys. And my mum and dad for being so supportive. I want to thank, Jenny, and you are like my best friend. You are not even like my publicists. I also want to thank, I also want to thank my manager, Melanie Greene, couldn't be here tonight. Mel, I am thinking of you, I love you so much. Steve and all of WME. I also, my goodness. Going blank, oh, okay. Shawn Levy for being one of the best I have ever had the pleasure of working with. Everything you taught me will carry on for the rest of my career. And lastly, I want to thank the Duffer Brothers. They created a badass, female iconic character that have got the honor to play. Thank you guys so much! I love you!"

(630) Millie said she really loves roast potatoes.

(631) Millie wore a custom Rodarte dress to the Stranger Things season three premiere.

(632) Stranger Things producer Shawn Levy said pairing David Harbour and Millie in season two was the Clash of the Titans. "You've got power going against power."

(633) In 2020, Millie made a tearful Instagram post in which complained about a fan who had kept filming her out shopping - despite Millie's request that she stop. "Why would anyone want to be taken a video of?" said Millie. "Of me? It's not like of the both of us. If I don't want to be taken a video of, I don't have to be. It just makes me upset when people try to push the boundary, and I just wish people were more respectful."

(634) Millie said Rachel is her favourite character in Friends.

(635) Millie said she would be open to appearing in an Eleven spin-off show after Stranger Things ends.

(636) It was humid and sticky in Georgia when they shot the Halloween trick or treat scenes in Stranger Things 2 so it became something of a challenge to make sure the kids didn't look hot or sweaty in any shots.

(637) When the first season of Stranger Things came out, Variety wrote that Millie had 'the kind of presence some actors take a lifetime to acquire. She is about to be cast in a lot of projects.'

(638) Jackson, Georgia often doubles for (the fictional) Hawkins in Stranger Things. Jackson is a small town between Atlanta and Macon.

(639) Benny's Burgers in the first season of Stranger Things is in reality Tiffany's Kitchen in Lithia Springs, Georgia. Tiffany's Kitchen is a real diner which you can go and eat in.

(640) Millie said she likes hoodies and baggy clothes when she's relaxing.

(641) When asked what her favourite red carpet outfit has been so far, Millie said - "It's hard to pin down just one moment, as so many have their own special meaning to me. If I had to choose, I guess I would say the Calvin Klein By Appointment look I wore to my first Emmys as a nominee in 2017. It was so special and everything I hoped for and envisioned for that experience."

(642) Millie wore a Dior gown to the London Godzilla premiere.

(643) Millie says Spotify is the most important app on her phone.

(644) Millie has a Mercedes car.

(645) Millie is a fan of the film Moulin Rouge.

(646) Millie has a Louis Vuitton handbag.

(647) Millie is a big fan of the Netflix movie Someone Great.

(648) Millie said if she ever made a biopic she would like to play Amy Winehouse.

(649) The Duffer Brothers said they had never watched the BBC America show Intruders when they cast Millie in Stranger Things. They cast Millie on the basis of her auditions rather than any previous work they had done.

(650) Millie is a fan of 90 Day Fiancé. This is a reality show.

(651) At her speech to the United Nations in 2019, Millie said - "At school, I was bullied by a group of students. I remember feeling helpless. School used to be a safe place. Now I was

scared to go. I didn't know who I could trust — who I could turn to. Like millions of other girls around the world, I've also been bullied and harassed online," she continued. "It's a terrifying feeling to look at your phone and see that the messages that people are sending you are filled with anger, hate and even threats. So many of these are from strangers. Anonymous trolls on the internet. Like all bullies, they gain their power by taking power away from others by making them feel as scared and helpless as I did. Somewhere in the world today — right now — a teenaged girl is being bullied online. She's scared. She's vulnerable. She feels alone. My message to her is this: you are not alone. There are people who care about you. There are people who will listen if you reach out for help. You have rights. I'm convinced that social media doesn't have to be a place of fear, bullying and harassment.

(652) When Eleven steals the eggo waffles from the store in season one of Stranger Things, there is a mistake because you can see some Trident gum as she leaves. This gum was not sold until 2001.

(653) The scene in Stranger Things 2 where Eleven shatters the windows in Hopper's cabin was done for real with no stunt double for David Harbour. "[The Duffers] had scripted flinging the dictionary, shoving the couch, but all those door slams and things were things we had to come up with as we were shooting it," said Shawn Levy. "Our special effects crew had to figure it out on the fly. [And that part with the windows blowing out] That's real. No visual effects. We rigged all the windows. [David Harbour even did it himself]. We had blocked it in a way — we knew he would be facing that door, and so we knew his faces would be protected, and he did NOT want to use stunt double, and so that was all real."

(654) Millie said that her mother is a great cook and makes fantastic gravy in particular.

(655) Millie says she would like to have more scenes with Joe Keery in Stranger Things. Joe plays Steve Harrington.

(656) When they reviewed the first ever episode of Stranger Things, Screenrant wrote - 'It's the young actors who carry a bulk of the emotional weight in the Stranger Things premiere, something they each pull off easily, bringing a real believability to their roles. From Will and his friends (Schnapp, Finn Wolfhard, Gaten Matarazzo, and Caleb McLaughlin) to the slightly older teenagers (Cara Buono, Charlie Heaton), all of the young cast feel like real kids, real people. Their performances are genuine, and it elevates the story at hand and gives a credibility to some of the truly bizarre happenings. Speaking of which, Brown's Eleven doesn't have a whole lot to do during the premiere, but she makes the most of her few scenes, earnestly portraying a lost, desperate girl one moment, and evoking a chilling menace the next. The transition is deceptively quick, and it may be the most terrifying part of the premiere, teasing the immensity of the strange power she possesses.'

(657) The scene in season one of Stranger Things where the kids hide in the bus at the junkyard became something of an ordeal for Millie and the crew because one of the boys broke wind.

(658) Millie uses castor oil for her eyelashes.

(659) Eleven's dress and wig costume from season one of Stranger Things is very similar to Paula - a character in the 1994 Super Nintendo classic Earthbound. Paula has psychokinetic powers too.

(660) Millie was a fan of water parks as a kid.

(661) Millie was given a friendship ring by Winona Ryder.

(662) When the boys and Eleven walk the train tracks in the woods during season one of Stranger Things this is an obvious reference to the film Stand By Me.

(663) Millie wore a Calvin Klein leather dress at the Stranger Things 2 premiere.

(664) Millie has a Audemars Piguet Royal Oak watch. She has no official connection with this brand so obviously just likes these watches.

(665) A popular (but eventually debunked) fan theory after season one of Stranger Things was that the Upside Down is a manifestation of the negative psychic emotions of Eleven.

(666) In the second episode of Stranger Things 2, there is a flashback where we see Eleven trapped in the Upside down wearing her famous Polly Flanders inspired dress from season one. The dress in the flashback was a duplicate because the original dress no longer fitted Millie.

(667) The Reebok sneakers Millie wears as Eleven in Stranger Things 3 were hard to find and purchased at a vintage Atlanta market.

(668) Eleven suggests she puts a sheet over her head and goes trick or treating as a ghost in Stranger Things 2. The kids in E.T. the Extra-Terrestrial do this with E.T in Spielberg's movie.

(669) Millie said that she once attended a BAFTA garden party and constantly introduced herself to the celebrities in the hope that Leonardo DiCaprio was there somewhere. Sadly though he wasn't.

(670) Millie says she exfoliates her face twice a week.

(671) The Hollywood Reporter said of Enola Holmes - 'Adapting the first of Springer's books as the origin tale in what's surely intended to be a series of Netflix movies, Harry Bradbeer's Enola Holmes makes a fine showcase for Stranger Things star Millie Bobby Brown, who gets to drop the layers of anxiety and trauma that make that show's El such a

compelling character. While no one will ever accuse the picture of overestimating its viewers' intelligence — Jack Thorne's script rarely misses the chance to drive a moral point home with one more pound to the head of the nail — it successfully imagines a place for its heroine in Holmes' world, then convinces young viewers that Enola needn't be constrained by that world's borders.'

(672) Asked to name his favourite scene in Stranger Things, Noah Schnapp chose the bike chase in season one where Eleven uses her powers to make the van fly over them.

(673) Eggo waffles were invented in San Jose, California, by three brothers, Tony, Sam, and Frank Dorsa. In 1953, the Dorsa brothers introduced Eggo frozen waffles to supermarkets throughout the United States.

(674) The Stranger Things kids watched the Superbowl teaser for Stranger Things 2 together.

(675) Netflix members voted Stranger Things as the top show that could be watched as a family.

(676) It took about five months to film the first season of Stranger Things.

(677) Millie owns a Fendi handbag.

(678) Universal Studios Hollywood created some Stranger Things themed treats to mark Halloween in 2019. These included Eleven's Waffle Sundae.

(679) Millie said - "Working on Stranger Things certainly opened my mind to the style and staples of the '80s, which has been a fun journey. The colours, the patterns, the volume. But I wouldn't say that I've woven that into my personal style much."

(680) Millie likes Ralph Lauren fashion.

(681) One of Millie's hobbies is buying luxury pajamas.

(682) Although she won an award, Millie couldn't attend the 2018 MTV awards because of her injured knee. In her videotaped acceptance message she addressed online trolls and bullying. "Since I know there are many young people watching this, and even to the adults too, they could probably use the reminder that I was taught – that if you don't have anything nice to say, then don't say it. There should be no space in this world for bullying, and I'm not going to tolerate it and neither should any of you. If you need a reminder of how worthy you are, and to rise above the hate, message me on Instagram."

(683) Millie is a fan of Disney World.

(684) Millie grows fruit and vegetables in her garden.

(685) When we see Max and Eleven discover the body in the bath in Stranger Things 3, this seems a lot like a homage to a similar scene in the film adaptation of Stephen King's The Dead Zone.

(686) Millie had 171 lines in Stranger Things 2. At the time of writing, this is the most amount of lines she has had in any season of the show.

(687) The Stranger Things kids performed Uptown Funk at their first Emmy Awards.

(688) The house in Atlanta where Millie's family lives cost nearly a million dollars. It was Millie's success as an actor that enabled the family to buy the house.

(689) Millie is a fan of Gucci bags.

(690) Millie is a fan of Mamma Mia.

(691) Millie won a Saturn Award for her role in Stranger Things.

(692) Millie said she is obsessed with carrots and can eat them with anything.

(693) According to a report in 2019, Millie earns an average of £87k per sponsored Instagram post.

(694) Millie had a low-key 17th birthday because of the COVID lockdown. She simply had a birthday cake at home.

(695) Millie said of her casting as Eleven - "I was living in London at that time. I was at my house, just watching TV, and my parents were like, "There's this show called Montauk. It's supposed to be really great. They haven't even written the first episode yet, but they want you to audition for it. It's going to be a good show." I was doing the tape for it, and I just loved it. They called me back, and I was doing another tape for them. They called me back again. They took that tape and then they were like, "Alright, we want to do a Skype meeting with you now." We didn't talk about the show once. We actually spoke about '80s movies and were talking about what my favourite things to do are, and what music I listen to. Then they were like, "Alright, we want you to fly to LA," and I was like, "Wow, okay. They must be serious about this now."

I went into the office and I saw one boy, one girl, Finn [Wolfhard], and then there was me. I went in with this other boy, and then the other boy left and Finn came in, and I was like, "Wow, Finn is way better than the other boy. Finn has to get this job." Then, we all got to experiment, and they just thought Finn and I were the perfect match to work with each other. The next day, on a Monday, they called me up and said, "Can you be our Eleven?" and I was like, "Yes, I can.""

(696) In the last quarter of 2017, Eggo consumption saw a 14% year-on-year increase thanks to Stranger Things.

(697) Waitresses at the Stranger Things 2 premiere were dressed in Eggo yellow uniforms.

(698) Eleven's use of television static in season two of Stranger Things is a reference to the 1982 horror film Poltergeist.

(699) Millie is a fan of the 1986 fantasy film Labyrinth. This film stars David Bowie and was made by Jim Henson of The Muppets fame.

(700) The car in the mall in Stranger Things 3 that Eleven throws at the baddies is a Chrysler Lebaron Convertible.

(701) When she visited Anfield Stadium in 2016, Millie attended a match between Liverpool and Manchester City.

(702) Millie is a big fan of strawberries.

(703) By the time that Stranger Things 2 came out, the glut of Stranger Things merchandise had snowballed into what you might expect of one of the most popular television shows in the world. You could soon buy Stranger Things t-shirts, Stranger Things jigsaw puzzles, Stranger Things Dungeons & Dragons, Stranger Things action figures, Stranger Things cardboard cut-outs, eggo waffle purses, a replica of Steve's baseball bat, Stranger Things candles, a Stranger Things Ouija board, and countless other items. Bars and cafes launched Stranger Things cocktails and Stranger Things pizza. There were a number of Stranger Things pop up bars around the world. Everyone wanted to celebrate the show. Stranger Things was a genuine global phenomenon that appealed to a broad spectrum of people and ages.

(704) Millie said she enjoyed it when her hair grew back after season one of Stranger Things because she was finally able to try out some new hairstyles again.

(705) Stranger Things 4 was unusual in that it began shooting for a few weeks but then had to shut down for several months

because of COVID. Millie said this was frustrating but health and safety was the most important thing.

(706) When she was a little kid, Millie wrote to Ellen asking if she could be a guest on her chat show. When she became famous, Millie appeared on Ellen for real and Ellen reproduced the letter Millie had written to her some years before.

(707) Millie said going to the Emmys for the first time was one of her most exciting experiences. Millie said she went star crazy and tried to meet as many celebrities as possible.

(708) Before Millie became famous, her family were so cash strapped trying to fund her acting ambitions that they had to borrow money off Millie's agent.

(709) Stranger Things was a global hit primarily because it was good but Netflix were also shrewd enough to dub and subtitle it into many foreign languages. For this reason Millie is now famous in many countries around the world.

(710) Millie said that red carpet events usually give her some anxiety.

(711) Millie said she didn't find it that difficult to learn an American accent for Stranger Things.

(712) When Millie's family ran into money troubles before she was famous, they had to move back to England from Florida. Money was so tight they had to move in with Millie's aunt. Millie was devastated by this because she thought her acting ambitions were over.

(713) The Duffer Brothers said it was a great relief when they found Millie because they were struggling to find a child actor capable of the raw emotion necessary to play Eleven.

(714) Millie said when she was growing up in England she was

a fan of the orange drink Capri Sun.

(715) There is a deleted scene in the first season of Stranger Things where Eleven reads out a line from Nancy's diary while she explores the Wheeler house alone. This scene was cut because Millie sounded too English when she read out the stipulated line. The line was "I love Steve".

(716) The Daily Beast wrote of Enola Holmes - 'Netflix's new mystery movie, Enola Holmes, showcases the full breadth of Millie Bobby Brown's talents with one of the entertainment industry's time-honored traditions: letting her do battle against the lung-crushing oppression of a corset. From the moment Brown crushed a Coke can with her brain as Eleven in Stranger Things, it was obvious she was going places. But the young actress's fascinating potential could only be revealed with time and a proper starring role. (And her feature debut, a supporting role in Godzilla: King of the Monsters, did not quite meet that mark.)

As Eleven, Brown has served as the emotional anchor for Stranger Things throughout its run. Over three seasons she has unravelled her mysterious and initially closed-off character into a delightfully normal (well, OK, kind of normal) tweenage girl—with all the crushes, insecurities, and temper tantrums that entails. But Eleven's taciturn nature has become visibly limiting as Brown grows into her raw talent—even as the character has slowly honed her speech skills. By shimmying into Enola's Victorian era garb, Brown sheds those constraints and embraces her chattier side. After three years playing a recovering telekinetic trauma survivor, it's... kind of refreshing to watch Brown simply play a teenage girl! Brown seizes her starring turn for all it's worth—narrating with humor and pluck as Enola outsmarts everyone around her.'

(717) Millie has joked that she would like to get some of the Stranger Things cast into the Enola Holmes sequel.

(718) Millie said it is a tradition in her family that they all have

Sunday dinner together.

(719) Millie's family originally moved to Florida to start a teeth whitening business.

(720) The Duffer Brothers think that no one could possibly have played Eleven as well as Millie has. They believe it was perfect casting.

(721) In Stranger Things 2, Millie got a solo spotlight episode called The Lost Sister but it wasn't very well received. The Lost Sister is the reason why Stranger Things 2 has nine episodes rather than eight. This episode takes us away from Hawkins and features Eleven in Chicago with Kali. None of the other regular cast members are in this episode (apart from a brief Hopper cameo). The Lost Sister is the closest that Stranger Things has come to having a bottle episode. A bottle episode in a TV show is usually an episode that doesn't advance the broader plot and is set in a constrictive location (like a stage play). Bottle episodes are usually deployed by TV shows when they need to save money.

The Lost Sister doesn't quite conform to these general rules in that it isn't especially constrictive but it does bring the momentum of the story in Stranger Things 2 to a halt. One of the biggest complaints about The Lost Sister was that we had to spend an entire episode in the company of (save for Eleven) characters that we didn't know and didn't really care about. The Duffers explained The Lost Sister as a character bottle episode. They felt that a concentrated focus on Eleven was required to complete her story. Shawn Levy would later admit The Lost Sister was an experiment that didn't quite work. The Lost Sister is easily the most unpopular episode of Stranger Things because it is so atypical of the show. It barely feels like an episode of Stranger Things at times. The general perception of The Lost Sister is that this detour simply wasn't strong enough as a piece of material or drama to exist in its own right as a complete isolated solo episode.

We have no investment in any of these characters apart from Eleven and so it is unavoidably difficult for us to care what happens to any of them.

(722) The Lost Sister's depiction of the Chicago skyline is too contemporary for 1984. The Trump International Hotel & Tower only opened in 2009 and the Blue Cross Blue Shield Tower was constructed in 1997.

(723) Eleven levitating and closing the dimension gate in the finale of Stranger Things 2 is a very Dark Phoenix inspired sequence. This was all done with green screen. The only thing that was actually there when the actors shot the scene was the shark cage. The increased amount of digital effects work in Stranger Things 2 made it feel a lot like shooting a Hollywood movie. The Duffers said they didn't especially enjoy shooting the sequence where the gate is closed by Eleven because it didn't feature any practical effects at all and it was disorienting to design and edit a sequence that only had green screen work as a backdrop. They said that the experience of this scene made the prospect of doing a big Hollywood movie awash in endless digital effects and green screen considerably less attractive. The scene was not much fun for the actors either. Millie almost vomited and David Harbour found the guns that Hopper had to use to be so loud they were deafening.

(724) Millie said one of the things that helped her to learn an American accent the most was watching Hannah Montana.

(725) The 'binge' option with Stranger Things was an integral part of its appeal and success. When a new season arrives, viewers can watch all of the episodes as quickly as they want. This is why so many episodes of Stranger Things end with a cliff-hanger. There is no frustration for the viewer because you don't have to wait a week to see what happens next. Shawn Levy has said that he would be disappointed if anyone DIDN'T binge Stranger Things. That's exactly what it was designed for.

(726) Eleven's hairstyle in Stranger Things 3 is similar to

Madonna's hair in the 1985 film Desperately Seeking Susan.

(727) Millie says that Kourtney is her favourite Kardashian.

(728) Millie says one of her favourite scents is rose.

(729) The first teaser trailer for Stranger Things 2 featured a real 1980 Eggo commercial.

(730) In their review of Enola Holmes, The Guardian wrote - 'It all rattles along amiably enough. Enola Holmes is the kind of all-star production that might once have been made by the BBC and graced the front cover of the Christmas Radio Times. Brown has a nice, easygoing way with the material, cheekily outpacing her famous brother Sherlock here and there and often doing fourth-wall breaks to smirk at the audience, and I loved Miss Harrison's steampunky motor car. But there should have been more specifically ingenious deducting and solving from Enola – codebreaking isn't the same thing. So ... is Moriarty's super-evil kid sister on the way?'

(731) According to Parrot Analytics, Stranger Things 3 registered 3.2 times the demand of Game of Thrones.

(732) Millie said when she made Godzilla: King of the Monsters she had to react to a tennis ball on a pole and pretend it was Godzilla. Godzilla was obviously added in later with digital special effects.

(733) Millie is a big fan of High School Musical.

(734) Millie said she quite likes oversized sweaters.

(735) Millie was seen snorkeling on the east side of Oahu, Hawaii during one of her days off from shooting Godzilla v Kong.

(736) Millie is a fan of Cookie Crisp. Cookie Crisp is a cereal made to recreate the taste of chocolate chip cookies.

(737) Millie said she still likes to do normal things like go to the grocery store. She said it would be far too exhausting to be a celebrity all the time.

(738) When Stranger Things was released in 2016, the Young Folks website wrote in their review - 'However, the biggest surprise performance of the entire cast has to be that of Millie Brown as Eleven. She absolutely nails the mysterious, yet childlike innocence of her character, and finding out the mysteries in Eleven's origins is what drives this season forward so well. Some of the scenarios where we discover her upbringing lead to the most heartbreaking moments throughout all the eight episodes, and even the most stone cold viewer will sympathize with the fragile, tender young girl.'

(739) Millie doesn't think Eleven would win in a battle against Godzilla.

(740) Millie has been on vacation to the Maldives.

(741) In their review of Stranger Things when it came out in 2016, the New Yorker wrote - 'Ryder's mirror is Millie Bobby Brown, who gives a career-launching performance as Eleven, the girl with something special—and who is, like Ryder's tomboy character in "Lucas," mistaken for a boy. Her head shaved, her face grave, she's silent for much of the series, but she bends the story toward her, through fearless emotional transparency. In one scene, she tiptoes into an older girl's bedroom, then opens a ballerina music box. Her eyes widen, and she takes shallow breaths, as if the music box were a bomb. It feels like no mistake that her nickname, El, is a soundalike for Elle. There's a risk, a very eighties one, that the character could become a contrivance, the exotic among the boys: E.T. in a skirt; she-Yoda. But Brown lends her an air of refugee devastation that makes her much more than the subject of someone else's fantasy, even when the dialogue threatens, once or twice, to lock her in a symbolic box.'

(742) Millie said she is quite scared of Pop Rocks. Pop Rocks are an American candy that pop in your mouth as they dissolve. She had to try some for a YouTube piece where she and the Stranger Things kids tested eighties toys and sweets.

(743) In 2020, Millie went on Instagram to display her Christmas Tree and decorations going up. Nothing strange about that you might think but it was actually October at the time! Millie obviously loves Christmas.

(744) The stunt in season one of Stranger Things where Eleven flips the lab van up in the air during the bike chase was achieved by nitrogen cannons (which fired a high-density plastic slug).

(745) Fans of Millie would probably concede that she doesn't get much in the way acting to do in the two Godzilla movies and they don't really represent the best use of her talents.

(746) Games Radar wrote of Stranger Things - 'The binge-watch series of the last few years. The Duffer brothers cobbled together a patchwork of '80s references then siphoned all of that into a killer plot about government experiments on members of a small town in Indiana. Things come to a head when a young lad, Will Byers, goes missing, causing his mother Joyce (Winona Ryder), the sheriff (David Harbour), and Will's friends to consider the strangest possibility – that there's a parallel world to ours replete with horrific monsters and demons simply itching to get at you. The whole cast is terrific (this writer personally was very pleased to see Winona Ryder back in the thick of it). However, it's the young leads who steal the show. Scurrying around Hawkins on their bikes in the dead of night and hunkering down in basements trying to find their missing pal, they will melt your hearts, especially Millie Bobby Brown as Eleven.'

(747) Eleven experiences the memories of other characters in Stranger Things 3. This could be a riff on the Christopher Nolan film Inception.

(748) It is very intentional in season one of Stranger Things that Eleven is given a yellow dress and blonde wig like E.T. It is also intentional that when Eleven and the boys are on bikes trying to escape from Brenner's team in Chevy vans, we think that Eleven will probably make the bikes levitate and 'fly' like they did in Spielberg's film. Instead, Eleven makes a van levitate to clear their path. This was the Duffers using pop culture nostalgia for misdirection.

(749) When Eleven levitates a Millennium Falcon toy in the first season of Stranger Things you can tell it isn't a 1983 period accurate toy because it doesn't have orange stickers to denote the Falcon's engines.

(750) Racheslsreviews.net wrote of the first season of Stranger Things - 'Millie Bobby Brown is also sensational as Eleven. She is mysterious and weird but not in the 'creepy child from horror movie' kind of way. You feel deeply sorry for her and much like Mike quickly want to protect her. It always seems like she is a hair away from bursting into tears but then she throws vans into the air. That mixture of strength and vulnerability really works.'

(751) In his review of Enola Holmes, Kim Newman wrote - 'As a period romp, this offers familiar pleasures – there is, of course, a sequence in which the plucky heroine hangs off the side of a speeding steam train while grappling with a hatchet-faced killer ... and several sequences hinge on the historical fact that there a segment of the suffragette movement learned jiu-jitsu to deal with police harassment during protests. The look owes a lot to Guy Ritchie's Holmes films, with nice CGI-assisted recreations of 1890s London — though it's a bit light on actual deduction and detective work since Enola mostly blunders into situations and wriggles out again at the convenience of the story. Partridge is surprisingly likeable in the potentially hazardous role of posh bloke love interest – basically playing the damsel in distress role while Brown handles all the kung fu – and there's a splendid turn from

Frances de la Tour as the marquess' dowager grandmother. It's not a classic – but it's undemanding, watchable stuff, and miles ahead of that Will Ferrell film. If you got through Sherlock Gnomes, you'll be okay with this.'

(752) The full text of Hopper's 'beyond the grave' letter to Eleven at the end of season three is - 'There's something I've been wanting to talk to you both about - and I know this is a difficult conversation. But I care about you both very much. And I know you care about each other very much and that's why it's important that we set these boundaries moving forward so we can build an environment, where we ALL feel comfortable, trusted and open to sharing our feelings. Feelings. Jesus. The truth is, for so long, I'd forgotten what those even were. I've been stuck in one place - in a cave, you might say. A deep dark cave. And then, I left some Eggos out in the woods and you came into my life and... for the first time in a long time, I started to feel things again. I started to feel happy. But lately, I guess I've been feeling... distant from you. Like you're pulling away from me or something. I miss playing board games every night, making triple-decker Eggo extravaganzas at sunrise, watching westerns together before we doze off.

But I know you're getting older, growing, changing. And I guess... if I'm being really honest, that's what scares me. I don't want things to change. So I think maybe that's why I came here, to try to maybe... stop that change. To turn back the clock. To make things go back to how they were. But I know that's naive. It's just... not how life works. It's moving. Always moving whether you like it or not. And yeah, sometimes it's painful. Sometimes it's sad and sometimes it's surprising. Happy. So you know what? Keep on growing up, kid. Don't let me stop you. Make mistakes, learn from 'em, and when life hurts you - because it will - remember the hurt. The hurt is good. It means you're out of that cave. But, please, if you don't mind, for the sake of your poor old dad, keep the door open three inches.'

(753) The Duffers didn't want 'Disney' kids when they were casting Stranger Things. They wanted to avoid child actors who seemed too arch, too showy, or too aware of the camera. They wanted kids who seemed authentic and felt like real children.

(754) Millie said - "I'm at work all day and doing stuff for everyone else and working on camera. Right before I go to bed, I do something I want to do, like watch a show or read a book or do something to take time for myself. I genuinely love spending time with my family, so I think those things keep me grounded and keep me appreciative and grateful for what I have."

(755) After the first season of Stranger Things came out, Ashley Hoffman of Time magazine recommended Eleven as a mascot for National Waffle Day.

'The young renegade had a rare and especially emphatic brand loyalty to Eggo waffles. Mike gave her her first waffle, so the breakfast treat may have represented belonging for her. When she has to survive without him, she heads straight to the supermarket to steal, what else? More. Waffles. Some ill-informed supermarket employee races to catch her, so she uses her to mind to slam the doors shut in his face. They shatter into a million pieces, and she blows out of the parking lot and never looks back. That's just what happens when you screw with Eleven's waffle stash.

On top of that, she loves the Kelloggs products so much, she'll even mess with frozen ones. Don't judge. It's not like the woods are full of toasters and outlets when you're an E.T.-themed fugitive who just checked out of Hawkins Lab and you'll do anything to survive. Which brings us, sadly to the show's finale. In the end, we see Chief Jim Hopper tucking away some waffles and some Christmas cookies in a secret forest box. In the ultimate sign that waffles and Eleven are inseparable, it's the waffles that tell everyone that Eleven is likely still around in some form.'

(756) Millie said that among the classic movies she watched in preparation for playing Eleven in Stranger Things were Close Encounters of the Third Kind and Poltergeist.

(757) When asked what her favourite outfit to wear was, Millie replied - "I know you wanted a really fancy answer there but I'm not going to give you one... onesies."

(758) Millie said she is a fan of the television show The Crown. The Crown is a historical drama series about the reign of Queen Elizabeth II.

(759) When asked where she would like to go if she could choose anywhere in the world, Millie said - "Bora Bora. No wifi. No signal. No Instagram, Twitter, texting. Nothing like that. I would just be secluded on an island with nothing to do. That's what I want to do." Bora Bora is an island group in the Leeward Islands. The Leeward Islands comprise the western part of the Society Islands of French Polynesia.

(760) Millie said that Gorillaz are among her favourite music artists.

(761) Film Fare wrote of Enola Holmes - 'The best part of this frothy take on the Holmes story is Millie Bobby Brown playing the charismatic younger sister. She talks constantly to the camera, giving a running commentary about what she feels and observes. It would have been irritating in the hands of a lesser actor but such is Bobby Brown's charm that you don't mind this constant chatter that she keeps with the audience. The film has a dishy Henry Cavill playing Holmes and it's to Bobby Brown's credits that she outshines the handsome actor in their scenes together.

Or it could be that Cavill, like a gentleman, let his younger colleague run away with the thunder. The film isn't about Sherlock, in any case, but about Enola. Despite all her training, she isn't worldly-wise as her brothers and the film serves as an origin story for the heroine. Watching the film, one tends to forget that Millie Bobby Brown is only 16. She's the Hollywood star to watch-out-for in the future. Her effortless acting makes you forget Sherlock. Suddenly, his mystique as an emotionless detective seems to be passe as you want to know more about his more dynamic sister. Fine beginnings indeed. The game, as they say, is afoot and going by the film's and Bobby Brown's popularity, we're in for some further adventures of Enola in time to come.'

(762) The makeup department on Stranger Things have different viscosities of fake blood for Eleven's nosebleeds to control how far it goes down Millie's face before it hits the lip.

(763) The magazines Millie has appeared in cover shoots for include Elle, Dazed, and Vogue.

(764) Millie said that she found Stranger Things quite scary when she was allowed to watch some of the first season footage for the first time. "Yeah, I really was scared. I was scared of myself. I was like, wow, "Eleven is evil." But yeah, the beginning bit, the boys were laughing at me, because I was sitting there, and we had this preview on the set. So we finished, I think it was (episode) three and four, and the directors were like, we have a screening tonight. I was like, "Yes, yes, I'm so happy!" So we all got together, the crew and everyone, we watched episode one and two, and the first episode... the scientist pops out, I jump up and I was like "No, oh my god! No" and the boys were like, "Chill out, Millie!" And I was like, "No, that's scary!"

And the demogorgon! Because once we were in the void, and the Duffers (the creators of "Stranger Things") like to tease me a lot because they're like my big brothers, and they ... I was in the void, and there was this monster sound that had to go off. I just thought, you know, that the first AD could go "roar," or something like that. No! They got sound department in, and they put speakers out, and it was like, "ROAR," and I ran! I was like, "help, help, I'm dying!" So yeah, I get scared very easily."

(765) Millie owns some Ugg slippers.

(766) Millie is a fan of Maroon 5.

(767) It needed 1,200 pounds of salt to make Eleven/Millie float in the kiddie paddling pool for The Bathtub.

(768) The Duffer Brothers estimate that they had around fifteen rejections before signing a deal with Netflix to make Stranger Things.

(769) Millie said that the kids on Stranger Things are always stealing one another's potato chips on the set.

(770) Millie said - "I immediately connected with Enola Holmes. I felt like I had found someone just like me. Growing up, I didn't see a young, female British lead on screen who I could relate to. After reading the book, I wanted to bring the story to life for my seven-year-old self. As a producer, I was able to provide creative input and see this film come to life in the way that I hoped and envisioned it would."

(771) Millie has a Shearling jacket.

(772) Millie is a fan of Karaoke.

(773) Millie said - "Style is constantly evolving, and my personal style is no exception. That's the beauty of fashion. Since I was a young girl, my style has ranged from boho chic to glamorous sparkles to comfy sweats and back again."

(774) When it comes to footwear, Millie has shown a fondness for Dr Martens boots.

(775) Steven Spielberg has praised Stranger Things and said he enjoys the show.

(776) Millie said she is a big fan of the late Whitney Houston.

(777) Millie said that during the COVID quarantine she watched the whole of Game of Thrones.

(778) Millie said that she and the other Stranger Things kids made a point of watching Finn Wolfard in the Stephen King horror film IT.

(779) Millie said - "Be yourself...there's nothing else. Why be anyone else? You can't be different. You are who you are. I think bettering yourself is always key. You're never going to be perfect, and you have to understand that, but I think by losing judgement, understanding that your flaws are actually some of your best qualities, and being kind to people... Something I stand by and what my mum and dad kind of brought me up with, is if you don't have anything nice to say, don't say it. And you can't change people. You can't change how people are, so if you remain yourself, then you won't be insecure about yourself. I'm definitely not an insecure person. I like who I am, I've been brought up that way, but I think bettering yourself and not judging people and loving people for who they are is key."

(780) The prehistoric bird picture that Eleven has on her wall in Stranger Things 3 was on the wall of the Wheeler basement in season one.

(781) Millie said she is a fan of The Society. The Society is an American mystery teen drama television series from Netflix. Millie must have disappointed though as it was cancelled after one season.

(782) Eleven wears a baby mask from Terry Gilliam's film Brazil in The Lost Sister.

(783) Millie is a big fan of Nike sneakers.

(784) Millie said that when she was shooting scenes for the

first season of Stranger Things she found it quite difficult to cry when it was cold. "I can't cry when it's cold. I went out into the quarry one night, and in the scene where we find Will's fake body, and we all come out and Mike's really upset with me, and I couldn't cry. I was like, "Cry!" I was like, "I'm not crying! I'm not crying!" And the boys were crying, and I'm like, "This is unbelievable." I'm going down the lake, just cry, cry. I'm listening to music, but I'm not crying. I'm not crying! So I've got to do something other than cry."

(785) Millie is a fan of cotton candy. Being English, she would probably call it candyfloss.

(786) Millie is a fan of the 1990s girl group TLC.

(787) Millie said that when the kids talked about Snapchat on the set of the first season of Stranger Things, Winona Ryder had no idea what they were talking about. Winona said she thought Snapchat was a brand of potato chips!

(788) Millie said that Angelina Jolie is an actress she looks up to. "She's iconic. She becomes her characters so beautifully, and she's actually an amazing person overall."

(789) In 2016, the Daily telegraph wrote of Stranger Things - 'Millie Bobby Brown continues to be the star of the show: she has inspired fan art and tattoos, a worldwide acknowledgment of Eggos, the waffles her character devours and given a whole new life to the phrase mouth breather.'

(790) Millie used to train at the Phoenix MMA gym in Bournemouth.

(791) Millie said she enjoys baking cupcakes.

(792) In the Stranger Things season one finale, Eleven kills some agents in a corridor and blood flows from their eyes. This gruesome touch is a homage to David Cronenberg's 1981 film Scanners.

(793) The passage from Anne of Green Gables that Hopper reads to Eleven in Stranger Things 2 is - 'I would feel so sad if I was a disappointment to her -- because she didn't live very long after that, you see. She died of a fever when I was just three months old. I do wish she'd lived long enough for me to remember calling her mother. I think it would be so sweet to say 'mother,' don't you? And father died four days afterwards from fever too. That left me an orphan and folks were at their wits' end, so Mrs. Thomas said, what to do with me. You see, nobody wanted me even then. It seems to be my fate.'

(794) The Duffer Brothers had to promise Netflix that the spectacular stunt in season one of Stranger Things where Eleven flips the van in the air would feature in the trailer.

(795) The first full trailer for Stranger Things 3 had 22 million views in one week on YouTube.

(796) One advantage Stranger Things 2 had was that the children in the cast didn't seem to have changed too much at all since season one. They still looked like little kids. This was no longer the case by the time Stranger Things 3 later went into production.

(797) Millie found she had a lot in common with Winona Ryder when they worked together on Stranger Things because Winona began her career as a child actor and was also famous for having very short hair in her youth.

(798) Although Millie had great success in the end, being a child actor is no picnic. Child actors will often find themselves competing with hundreds of other children for a part. Millie experienced this herself in her early rejections. If the Duffer Brothers and Stranger Things had not come along there is no guarantee that Millie, despite her talent, would have made it as an actor.

(799) When asked about the end of Stranger Things, Millie

said - "I would love Eleven's story to be rounded off by like a good ending. I trust the Duffer brothers so much that it's going to be beautiful and I'm going to love it no matter what it is."

(800) In 2018, Millie and her Stranger Things co-star Gaten Matarazzo sent messages of support to a young boy who threw a Stranger Things party that no one turned up to.

(801) Although Millie isn't the biggest fan of shopping she seems to make an exception in the case of Christmas shopping.

(802) Regarding her makeup range, Millie said - "I came up with the idea for my beauty range when my dad and I were on a plane from Atlanta to Argentina. I was practising applying make-up – I'm a bit of a fanatic – and while I looked great, I didn't feel great. I told my dad I felt there was a gap in the market for skincare and make-up aimed solely at young people. I knew I could create something that sat in the middle and "spoke" to people like me and my friends. Something that's healthy and good for your skin, but also fun and still represents youth.

As soon as we landed, I phoned everyone and said I had to do something of my own.' Fast-forward two years and Millie has created a range of 15 products, including skincare and cosmetics. It has chic, matte purple packaging – her favourite colour – and a fragrance that's a mix of lavender, rose and cucumber, her favourite scents. 'As a young person and entrepreneur, I wanted to be taken seriously. And it's been hard, these past six years, working non-stop to prove to myself and to society that young people deserve a seat at the table."

(803) Millie said she watches All American. This is a Netflix drama about American Football.

(804) When season one of Stranger Things came out, Millie said she was rather perplexed by the Upside Down void in the show. "Do you know I'm still kind of processing what it actually means? Upside down, I still don't even get it. I don't

understand it though, and people are like, "Everybody else does! Why don't you?" And I'm like, "I want to, but I don't." I know what the upside down is, but the void? It's my mind? Me and Winona (Ryder, who plays Joyce Byers) are like, I don't understand. We've given up."

(805) The Duffer Brothers have said Akira was an influence on Eleven and Stranger Things. Akira is a 1988 Japanese animated film based on a comic. Akira is set in a future Tokyo and features psychics, telepathy, telekinesis, and secret government labs.

(806) Regarding the kiss between Mike and Eleven in the first season finale of Stranger Things, Millie said - "It was, like, my first kiss, so it was kind of weird. But then, like, when I'd done it, I thought, Wow. It makes sense for the storyline."

(807) Millie is set to star in a film adaptation of The Thing About Jellyfish. The Thing About Jellyfish is a 2015 children's book by Ali Benjamin and the story of a girl named Suzy who becomes convinced that her friend's accidental drowning was the result of a rare jellyfish sting and not just a random tragedy.

(808) Millie said she was twelve years-old and in Palm Springs when a fan asked to have a photo taken with her for the first time.

(809) Millie said - "You need to put yourself in a happy space. And make sure that you love yourself and that you're doing things that are ultimately going to make you happy. And once you do that first, then you will find your self-confidence and self-love throughout that journey."

(810) Millie was born in Spain because her British grandparents ran a restaurant there and Millie's family decided to be closer to them.

(811) Millie has a crush on the actor Timothée Chalamet.

(812) Millie and Sadie Sink nicknamed themselves Ketchup and Mustard on the set of Stranger Things 3 because the red and yellow raincoats that Eleven and Max wear during the rainstorm episode.

(813) The Fury, a 1978 supernatural thriller directed by Brian De Palma, was an influence on Stranger Things. Adapted from the novel of the same name by its own author, John Farris, The Fury revolves around a secret area of the government's intelligence department trying to forge a division of super powered humans who have telekinesis.

(814) Millie's birthday is on February the 19th.

(815) Millie says that she loves unicorns.

(816) Of her dogs, Millie said in 2020 - "I have the two mini poodles that drive me insane. The other one is Winnie, who is sat on the table right now – she is Posh Spice to the max – she knows her angles. I have six dogs in total. We have a mini cavapoo who lives in London called Nora, a mini goldendoodle called Leo and then we have, Ronnie and Reggie – two English mastiffs, they're huge – who are named after the Kray twins because we think that they're like English gangsters. We thought they were going to be the guard dogs, but they freak out at thunder – they are wimps."

(817) Millie said that when the COVID lockdowns began she quite enjoyed sleeping late and having lots of spare time but in the end she got bored and wanted to go back to work.

(818) Millie said she likes to eat popcorn when she watches scary movies.

(819) Millie said she finds it really annoying when people make a lot of noise while eating food.

(820) Millie said - "My skincare routine constantly changes

depending on what I have scheduled for the day - if I'm on set, at a shoot, or just hanging out at the house. I try to always stay consistent by at least washing my face with the Clean Magic Face Wash, moisturising with the Dreamy Dew Moisturiser, and applying an SPF. Then depending on if I have more time in the morning, I might add in a toner, face mask, or special treatment."

(821) Millie has created her own line of Converse sneakers.

(822) Millie was excited to meet Matt Smith at an awards show. Matt Smith was (appropriately enough) the eleventh Doctor in Doctor Who.

(823) During the production on season one of Stranger Things, Millie's little sister put on a talent show for David Harbour and Winona Ryder.

(824) Millie is a fan of the board game Monopoly.

(825) Georgia made a great production base for Stranger Things because the area had an eclectic mix of scenary from gorges to forests to Spielbergian towns.

(826) Millie is a fan of fish and chips. This is a traditional fast food takeaway dish in Britain.

(827) After season one of Stranger Things came out, Millie was asked what she thought the missing Eleven might be doing in the Upside Down. Millie said - "She's with Joyce's dog. She's grooming the dog in the void. Yup. She's having a mani-pedi with the demogorgon, stuff like that. But I have no idea, really."

(828) It is believed that Millie had her teeth straightened with Invisalign braces.

(829) Millie said that being the producer on Enola Holmes made her quite nervous at first. "I was very nervous. I'm not

going to lie. I've never done that before so to be honest I wasn't coming onto set like, 'I have authority.' I came on set like, 'Should I say this? Should I say that?' It was always nerve-racking because I've just never done that before. But as soon as I walked on to set, I didn't even have those thoughts come into my head. I just said, 'Oh, should we try this, or should we try that?' It just naturally came to me; it was such an amazing opportunity for me to learn and grow. I love putting my input in and have it been appreciated and listened to."

(830) Project MKUltra features heavily in the story of Eleven in season one of Stranger Things. From 1953 to 1973, the CIA funded experiments in order to learn how to control people for the purposes of spying. These experiments were designed to see if the human mind could be altered or controlled. The psychedelic drug LSD was a big part of the experiments and sensory deprivation chambers were used. The origins of the project are thought to have come from a fear that the Soviet Union was much more advanced in brainwashing techniques.

This was a sphere of the Cold War that America was apparently losing and so was born (after several similar if smaller projects) MKUltra. For the CIA, the worst-case scenario was that the Soviet Union could find a way to mindcontrol US military and intelligence officials. It all sounds somewhat crazy but experiments in psychological techniques were very real. The experiments included attempts to 'remote control' people for the purposes of manipulating agents in the field through electrical brain triggers. Obviously, the concept of anyone gaining super powers through MKUltra experiments is pure fantasy.

(831) Millie said her favourite line in Stranger Things 3 was when Eleven said to Mike Wheeler "I dump your ass!"

(832) Although it is sometimes suggested that the first season of Stranger Things operated on a modest budget this is not really true. At $6 million an episode, the first season cost around $50 million. While this is modest compared to big

Hollywood movie blockbusters, $6 million an episode is fairly high end for a TV show - especially a brand new one with no track record to speak of.

(833) The Duffers Brothers said that Millie listened to the Beasts of No Nation soundtrack to get in the right frame of mind for the big reunion scene between Eleven and Mike in Stranger Things 2.

(834) Millie is a fan of Cardi B.

(835) Millie said of the character Enola Holmes - "She's brave, vulnerable, honest and witty. Plus, she's a people person. Her story is about how she is afraid of being alone, and in the end, she finds her purpose in life. That's the story of growing up. I've gone through that. It resonates with me in so many ways."

(836) Millie's new Netflix deal is said to be for ten years.

(837) Millie said that when she went back to Atlanta to make Stranger Things 2 she was quite annoyed that her record player was left in England. She managed to get it shipped over in the end though.

(838) Millie said she quite likes the idea of doing a cookbook one day.

(839) The walkie-talkies the kids use in Stranger Things had a radius of about one mile. In the early 1980s they were mostly used by construction crews on building sites.

(840) Eleven was supposed to wear an ordinary bathing costume in the season one lab sensory deprivation water tank scenes in Stranger Things but the costume department had the idea of Eleven's lab bathing suit being designed as a more scientific or military costume. They added special 'floating' blocks to the suit.

(841) The props department and set decorators have to find a

lot of vintage (and sometimes defunct) brands to populate the backdrops in Stranger Things. Everything you see in the background in season one, be it washing powder, coffee, beer, potato chips, or soda, have to seem authentic to the 1980s.

(842) One of the most difficult scenes to shoot in season one of Stranger Things was the stunt where Eleven levitates the Chevy scientist van during the cycle chase. The stunt went wrong and destroyed a camera. Netflix gave the Duffers the go ahead (and funding) to try the stunt again and this time it went without a hitch.

(843) Sadie Sink said she never previously had much interest or aptitude for makeup herself but has learned a lot about beauty care and makeup from her friendship with Millie.

(844) The first season of Stranger Things was produced in relative obscurity. There wasn't much buzz about the show and aside from Winona Ryder and Matthew Modine no one had heard of most of the cast. That all changed when they started shooting Stranger Things 2. Overheard drones buzzed the set trying to capture footage and Millie and the kids were now famous around the world.

(845) Matthew Modine is the villain of the first season of Stranger Things as Dr Brenner (aka Papa to Eleven). Dr Brenner might be mean to Eleven but Millie and Matthew Modine got on great. Millie said she had a nice family dinner with Matthew Modine during the shooting of season one.

(846) There seems to be little doubt that Millie has adapted to fame more comfortably than most people do. While it hasn't all been plain sailing she genuinely seems to have embraced and enjoyed the spotlight and opportunities afforded to her by the incredible success of Stranger Things.

(847) At the end of Stranger Things 2, when Dr Owens gives Hopper the legal documentation to adopt Eleven, the birth certificate lists Eleven's name as Jane Hopper.

(848) In one of the Stranger Things spin-off novels, it is stated that Dr Brenner had Eleven's real father drafted into the Vietnam War - where he was killed in the fighting.

(849) The music box in the Wheeler house plays Brahms' Lullaby in season one of Stranger Things when Eleven opens it.

(850) When she had to have her hair cut to play Eleven, Millie was also shown a photo of Natalie Portman in the film V for Vendetta. Natalie Portman had to shave her head for part of that film. Millie thought Natalie Portman looked pretty good with short hair so the thought of shaving her own hair suddenly didn't bother her so much.

(851) Eggo waffles come in a variety of flavours. Homestyle, buttermilk, blueberry, strawberry, cinnamon and brown sugar, chocolate chip, oats and berries, whole wheat, and gluten-free. Millie said she has only tried a few of these because she doesn't really eat Eggos in real life.

(852) Millie says that she finds people chewing gum rather annoying sometimes.

(853) The Guardian were not very impressed by Godzilla: King of the Monsters in their review. 'The tussle for power between giant monsters and humans is a timeless theme, tackled by the likes of Transformers, Jurassic Park and Pacific Rim franchises with varying degrees of success. The problem with Hollywood's latest take, Michael Dougherty's reimagining of the Japanese studio Toho's famous kaiju series, is not its predictability, but its utter gracelessness. The plot picks up after 2014's Godzilla. A sonar device developed by Vera Farmiga's Emma to control the monsters has been hijacked by an eco-terrorist; her ex-husband (Kyle Chandler) is drafted in to track it down. Their teenage daughter (Millie Bobby Brown from Stranger Things) is a distraction, caught in the middle of her divorced parents. Battle scenes occur in weather

conditions so extreme that the action is rendered indecipherable (as are the beloved giant creatures, including the three-headed serpent King Ghidorah, bird-like Rodan and winged Mothra). The ugly visual effects are outdone only by the sound design, which is relentlessly loud and thunderingly tedious. Verbal exchanges between the humans are devoid of wit and barely functional in communicating the story.'

(854) Millie likes brown sugar in her latte. She said she got a taste for coffee at quite a young age.

(855) Millie usually has her phone in Cloud Lavender.

(856) Millie said - "I think as young people, we go through a phase of using makeup to cover up or fit in, but when you learn to love yourself you start using makeup to experiment with your identity and express different sides of your personality in a really fun way. One day you might feel like wearing a strong, powerful look or going really fresh-faced and neutral, while another day you might feel like getting all glammed up or doing big '80s statement makeup."

(857) Millie is a fan of the singer Lizzo.

(858) Millie quite often posts makeup free pictures on Instagram.

(859) Millie is pretty remarkable in that she became the main breadwinner in her family when she was about twelve years-old.

(860) Millie's makeup range includes a melon scented face wash.

(861) Millie likes baking chocolate brownies.

(862) In 2020, Millie was seen on Instagram at home wearing a Wigan Warriors shirt. Wigan Warriors are an English rugby league team. The reason Millie was wearing the shirt is

because she was dating Joseph Robinson at the time. Joseph is a player at Wigan Warriors.

(863) When she was growing up in England, Millie mostly lived in the Winton area of Bournemouth.

(864) Millie is generally regarded to have been the highest paid child star in the world circa 2017. These days she would to be ranked on teen star wealth lists.

(865) Gemma Hill, who was Millie's primary school teacher in England, said of Millie - "She loved any kind of performance, she would always come in quite excitedly around the time of Britain's Got Talent and I think, although I'm not sure, she may even have entered at one point. You could see she had the quality, the ambition and the drive; she knew that performing was what she wanted to do and she loved being on stage, singing and dancing."

(866) Millie is a variant of the Latin and Old German name Amelia, the Latin names Camilla and Kamilla, the Greek name Melissa, the Old English name Mildred, and the Old French name Millicent.

(867) On shaving her hair to play Eleven, Millie said - "I need to show how much I'm involved with this character and how much I'm involved with the show. I wanted the best for the show and if that's what I had to do, then that's what I had to do!"

(868) The raincoats Max and Eleven have in Stranger Things 3 were felt by some horror fans to be an easter egg pertaining to the Nicholas Roeg film Don't Look Now.

(869) Millie is a fan of watermelon.

(870) Vox was not terribly impressed by Godzilla: King of the Monsters in their review. 'King of the Monsters feels like a cruelly cynical example of a blockbuster cash-in with no heart,

an assembly-line product, the movie equivalent of indistinct, high-sodium corn chips designed to fly off the convenience store rack to satisfy hunger pangs, only to be forgotten an hour later. In exchange for your money, they'll feed you the least they possibly can. (The difference here is that movie theaters want to charge you a lot of money to see the latest blockbuster, rather than just a buck or two for a snack.) Corn chips are fine. But if you subsist on corn chips alone, you'll end up sick.'

(871) Millie is a fan of the vintage Swedish pop group ABBA.

(872) Millie said she was about ten when she became interested in makeup - although she was obviously too young to use too much of it at the time.

(873) Millie said she uses eye balm to avoid puffiness around the eyes after an exhausting flight.

(874) Millie likes making pancakes.

(875) At the start of 2020, Millie posted a social media picture of herself near Bournemouth Pier. This suggested she had gone back to her old home town in England to visit relatives.

(876) The AV Club wrote of the first season of Stranger Things - 'What the Duffers lose in originality they make up for in the assured execution. The sibling team co-wrote and/or directed most of the episodes, and it's the rare example of a freshman television series that knows exactly what it wants to be from its earliest frames. The direction and cinematography are stunning throughout, and the series nails all the appropriate period details from the costumes to the creepy production design. There's also the irresistible, Imaginary Forces-designed title sequence, which is rendered with vintage fonts and mottled with faux film grain. Balancing style and substance is always challenging for a series like Stranger Things, but the show is perfectly calibrated. It feels like watching a show produced during the era in which it's set, but with the craft of today's prestige television.'

(877) Millie has recieved 26 award nominations for her role as Eleven in Stranger Things.

(878) One of Millie's favourite holiday destinations is Mexico.

(879) The girls that Eleven gets revenge on at the mall in Stranger Things 3 by making an orange drink explode are the same girls that were mean to Dustin at the Snow Ball dance in Stranger Things 2 when he was looking for someone to dance with.

(880) When the toys belonging to Dustin come to life (in reality it is Eleven using her powers) in Stranger Things 3, this scene is similar to a scene in the 1985 Roland Emmerich fantasy film Making Contact.

(881) The Glasgow Guardian wrote of Enola Holmes -

'Millie Bobby Brown carries the movie on her own for much of the runtime, and she's quite capable of doing so. Since Stranger Things, it's been obvious that she has a particular screen presence, and that her acting skills are pretty good. Enola's mystery-solving skill takes its cues from the typical Sherlock style but avoids the hyper-focus and detail-oriented nature seen in Robert Downey Jr or Benedict Cumberbatch's versions of the character (Cavill's performance does pastiche this to a degree).

Rather, she focuses more on codes and cyphers, and on disguise. This knack for disguise gives Brown plenty of opportunities to try on a variety of costumes throughout the movie. Enola is also scrappy and resourceful, so Brown gets up to a lot of mischief in the role. Despite its flaws, the film is solid, pure escapism — and isn't that what we all need right now? Don't go in expecting it to reinvent Sherlock Holmes; it has nothing so profound to say. But you can certainly go in expecting to be taken on a fun romp through upper-class England in the late 19th century, and enjoy the mystery that the story sets up.'

(882) Stranger Things producer Shawn Levy said that when you cast child actors you audition the famalies as much as you audition the kids. He said they prefer to cast kids who have supportive and grounded relatives.

(883) Millie said she likes to watch Liverpool play football but it's a bit difficult when she's in the United States because the games usually start at some bizarre hour like four in the morning American time.

(884) Millie is a fan of the late singer John Lennon.

(885) Millie has worn ribbons to promote the American Civil Liberties Union and the Gay and Lesbian Alliance Against Defamation (GLAAD) Together movement.

(886) Millie said of her parents' financial struggles before she made it big - "There were times we didn't know if we could afford food or pay the rent. It was very hard. There were lots of tears."

(887) Entertainment Weekly wrote of the Enola Holmes movie - 'Millie Bobby Brown is cheeky and spritely in the role. As an actress, she has a self-possessed quality that grounds the performance. Enola is bright and capable, but she's also still a teenager, a woman finding her way in the world in spite of (or perhaps because of) a profound sense of loneliness. Brown calibrates this all with ingenuity, juggling the shades of her emotional state with such aplomb you need Holmesian powers of observation to catch them all.'

(888) According to a wage indicator website in 2020, Millie makes about $90,000 a week from her various contracts.

(889) In 2019, Millie was the 37th most popular name for baby girls in England.

(890) Millie is a fan of the 1990s girl group The Spice Girls.

(891) Eleven's powers in Stranger Things derive from her mother Terry Ives being part of an MKUltra program. Dr Brenner stole Eleven from Terry Ives and covered it up as a miscarriage. Terry tried to get Eleven back but Brenner stopped her and gave Terry Ives electro shock treatment so she couldn't speak anymore.

(892) Millie is a fan of baked beans. This is a traditional English comfort food.

(893) There were reports in 2020 that Millie was about to release a music album but these articles turned out to be somewhat premature. At the time of writing Millie has yet to release a music album and her focus seems firmly on acting.

(894) Spectrum Culture wrote of Millie's Enola Holmes movie - '

The charming and zippy detective caper Enola Holmes, directed by Harry Bradbeer, displays its most potent ingredient right off the bat: Millie Bobby Brown, in the title role, looking straight through the screen and saying, "Where to begin?" She continues to break the fourth wall throughout the film, enlisting the audience's sympathy in her adventures. The technique starts off as a vehicle for quick exposition but evolves into a suggestion of something deeper, hinting at revealing her subconscious mind where the legendary Holmes intellect is hard at work deciphering mysteries.

The film's running joke is that teenage Enola is even sharper than her famous older brother, Sherlock (Henry Cavill), who pops in from time to time only to be outwitted by his little sister. Brown is disarming in her vulnerability and wit, although the family-friendly PG-13 rating ensures that nothing gets too dark or racy even as the thoughts she shares touch on her famous family's secrets. It could be that her access to an unseen audience in her mind is the key to the empathy that sets her apart from her brilliant but prickly older brother. If so, she might prove to be an even greater detective. It doesn't take a magnifying glass to detect the traces of aspiring franchise in Enola Holmes, and her continuing adventures might prove to be as durably engaging as Sherlock's.'

(896) Finn Wolfhard said his kiss with Millie in season one of Stranger Things wasn't his first kiss. Millie teased him about this and said it probably was his first kiss.

(897) Screen Rant ranked Eleven as the second most likeable character in Stranger Things. Steve Harrington topped the poll.

(898) For the Christmas scenes at the end of season one of Stranger Things, the production crew had to import large amounts of ice and powder to Atlanta create a realistic winter landscape.

(899) One theory for why the Duffers got over a dozen rejections when they first tried to pitch Stranger Things is that there had been a number of underwhelming television shows and miniseries based on the stories of Stephen King. The prospect of another show heavily inspired by Stephen King evidently wasn't an appealing prospect to many executives.

(900) At the time of writing, Millie has won ten awards for her performance as Eleven in Stranger Things.

(901) When Eleven encounters a fiery fantastical farm tornado in Stranger Things 3 this is a reference to Dorothy in The Wizard of Oz.

(902) Doux reviews wrote of season one of Stranger Things - 'The best member of the young cast was by far and away Millie Bobby Brown (great name) as Eleven. She had a ton of story to carry pretty much by herself, and she was consistently endearing as well as terrific at projecting her character's "otherness." She made me want to beat up anyone who had

ever used and abused Eleven, which I'm pretty sure was the point.'

(903) Kiss.ie reviewed the face wash and eye balm from Millie's Florence by Mills beauty collection. Their verdict was - 'The face wash is gentle and has a gorge natural smell of cucumber and rose. It's great if your face is feeling a bit tight or if you're starting out your skincare routine, it's got loads of natural ingredients, so if you're sensitive, it might be a good one to try. It doesn't sting or feel too strong on the skin and leaves your skin feeling soft and clear.

It is PERFECT for those of us who don't wear too much makeup on a daily basis and want to remove it in a gentle way. I'd recommend using a cleaning mitt or face cloth to remove it, rather than tissue – which it says on the box. It just makes for a more even removal and can feel a bit softer on your skin for an all-found gentle experience. I found it really easy to apply and spreadable, so you don't need to use too much of it. Would buy again. The eye balm feels lovely and cool on the skin with its curved metal tip, especially if you're feeling tired. Be careful not to use too much product as you only need a small amount to spread all around your under eye. If you're a concealer fan, it's a great alternative if you're looking to wear less makeup (or your school doesn't allow makeup) but you still want to brighten up that area.'

(904) The BFI website wrote of the Enola Holmes movie - 'The mantle of master detective is here taken up by Enola – who also inherits her older brother's absent wit – with the audience playing Watson when Millie Bobby Brown addresses the camera with a sly remark or an askance eye roll. Brown is tasked with much more than recreating the usual brand of Holmesian intellectual snoopery, however, with Enola's childhood Jujitsu lessons frequently coming in handy in encounters with baddies. It's a remarkable performance from the young virtuoso, who carries much of the film's weight on her shoulders without an on-screen gang or sidekick to accompany her; she is both the emotional and the comedic

core of the story and juggles these dual responsibilities deftly. Without a consistent cast to bounce quick gags off, the fourth-wall-breaking moments are a vital vein of light relief, even if some jokes, clearly aimed at a young crowd, are grating to an adult ear. The funniest setups involve changes in disguise – including into a street urchin and a mourning widow – which allow Enola moments of playfulness whilst further highlighting her subversion of strict Victorian gender roles.'

(905) In 2017, Millie was trapped in Bali for six days thanks to the erupting volcano Mount Agung. She was on her way back from Australia at the time and because of the volcano disrupting all travel her four day visit to Bali turned to ten days. It wasn't a tremendous hardship though because she was staying in a five star hotel.

(906) Millie said she is scared of thunder and lightning and doesn't like loud noises. "I'm terrified of thunder and lightning," she said in 2021. "So, I'm very much normal in that respect. I don't like sleeping in the dark. I don't like loud noises — especially on set. I've recently been just terrified of anything that's like, 'Ba boom!"

(907) Bernie Hayes, who appeared in Godzilla v Kong with Millie, said Millie would sometimes bark like a dog before a take to give herself energy! "In between takes, would literally sing our hearts out. It was a lot of fun. She also likes to bark. I don't know if that was like a moment for her, like a period of a time where she was just into barking. But she would just bark like before a take, if she needed energy, she would just go, "woof, woof, woof, woof". I've seen a lot worse from actors."

(908) Millie said she was disappointed when she learned that Eleven was leaving Hawkins with the Byers family at the end of Stranger Things 3. "I read the script and I was like, "What, how is this even possible? Why are they moving away?" They were like "Didn't you read episode 3?" And I was like, "Oh yeah." Because Joyce said she wanted to move away from Hawkins. I don't know, I just felt really against it."

(909) Millie's mother did not want Millie to shave her hair to play Eleven in Stranger Things. Millie's mother, though understandably upset at the thought of her daughter's long hair being cut off, was obviously wrong about this in the end as cutting her hair off and playing Eleven made Millie not only famous but also a millionaire. And as Millie pointed out to her mother, hair does actually grow back!

(910) Clinical psychologist Dr Renee Carr believes that 'binging' shows like Stranger Things unlocks pleasure receptors in the brain. "When engaged in an activity that's enjoyable such as binge watching, your brain produces dopamine. This chemical gives the body a natural, internal reward of pleasure that reinforces continued engagement in that activity. It is the brain's signal that communicates to the body, 'This feels good. You should keep doing this!' When binge watching your favorite show, your brain is continually producing dopamine, and your body experiences a drug-like high. You experience a pseudo-addiction to the show because you develop cravings for dopamine."

(911) The Stranger Things kids handed out peanut butter and jelly sandwiches to celebrities at the 2016 Emmy awards.

(912) Millie has made light of often being cast as the slightly spooky troubled child

(913) Millie says that Gaten Matarazzo is the biggest prankster on the set of Stranger Things.

(914) Millie said that one thing she really loves to do is decorate her bedroom.

(915) When the first two episodes of Stranger Things were made available to critics in 2016, Wicked Horror wrote - 'One to watch is Millie Bobby Brown as the mysterious Eleven. Brown delivers a quiet, yet incredibly strong performance as a damaged young girl with ties to both the laboratory and the

town's residents.'

(916) Millie's parents say that the way they've coped with her immense fame is to try and make Millie's home life feel as normal and down to earth as possible.

(917) Enola Holmes was really the first time that Millie got a chance to be funny and show more of her range as an actor. It proved she was versatile and had enough charisma to play the lead.

(918) The August 2021 teaser for Stranger Things 4 revealed that Eleven, when it comes to her hairstyle, has some bangs. Being from England, Millie would call this a fringe.

(919) Millie says that she always watches a film if the trailer makes her cry.

(920) Millie's father said that after one of her first auditions as a child actor for a commercial, a casting agent took him to one side afterwards and told him he had a very unique daughter.

(921) Millie said it was fun to appear on This Morning and other morning magazine shows in Britain as a guest because she used to watch these shows before she was famous.

(922) Although Stranger Things is a horror themed show, Millie is quite rare among the cast for liking horror movies. Charlie Heaton, Natalia Dyer, Sadie Sink, Priah Ferguson, and Winona Ryder have all said that they don't watch horror movies in real life.

(923) In reality, the U.S Department of Energy obviously doesn't experiment with super powered children and open up dimensions to other realities. Paul Lester, who worked for the U.S Department of Energy (and is a Stranger Things fan too), wrote - 'Stranger Things depicts the Energy Department as a federal agency confronting terrifying monsters lurking in different dimensions. We don't mess with monsters, but the

Energy Department is in the business of detecting invisible dangers. Energy Department scientists throughout the country create new technologies that help prevent terrorists from getting their hands on nuclear materials. For example, Sandia National Laboratories developed a mobile scanner that can be used in shipping ports around the world to quickly detect radiological materials hidden inside massive cargo containers.'

(924) Eggo waffles were called Froffles when they first appeared in supermarkets.

(925) Charlie Heaton said he was amazed at how tall the children (now teenagers) in Stranger Things had become when season three began production. "As for the kids, when Stranger Things began, they were ten or eleven but they are growing into their adolescence now. They get so much taller, every year I come back. It's crazy watching them all grow up and seeing them all handle the success is incredible. They grow up and they grow up fast."

(926) In a 2019 poll by MoffettNathanson, Stranger Things was voted the second best Netflix show. It was beaten by Orange Is the New Black.

(927) The mall montage featuring Max and Eleven in Stranger Things 3 was supposed to include a food feast and the girls getting their ears pierced but these scenes were not included in the end.

(928) The dimensional rift story in season one of Stranger Things has many influences but perhaps the most obvious one is Stephen King's novella The Mist (which was later turned into a decent film by Frank Darabont). The story in The Mist has a town engulfed in a strange monster laden mist after a military experiment goes wrong.

(929) Millie says she is a fan of meditation.

(930) The Lucky Chip restaurant in London brought out some

Stranger Things themed dishes in 2016 to celebrate the show. The dishes included the Eggos Waffle burger and Eleven's Onion Rings.

(931) The endless Stranger Things stuff you can now buy includes a Demogorgon dog hat and a Waffle purse.

(932) Because the character of Eleven doesn't say much at all, Millie had to largely act with her eyes and face but still delivered a heart-rending performance.

(933) For her seventh birthday, Millie went swimming with dolphins.

(934) Millie says she can do the Hoedown Throwdown. This is a dance in Hannah Montana: The Movie.

(935) Millie said - "I grew up drawing on my sneakers to personalize them and make them my own."

(936) YouTube user Stryder used the Deepfake technology to replace Carrie Fisher with Millie as Princess Leia in a selection of scenes from the original Star Wars movies. It was amazing how much Millie looked like the young Princess Leia.

(937) There has been speculation that Millie, despite only being 17 (at the time of writing), has had lip fillers injected into her lips. It could be though that this is simply a case of her pouting in photographs and people putting 2 and 2 together and coming up with five.

(938) Millie's Twitter (which she has since deactivated) got a 105% boost in followers in 2017 after Stranger Things 2 came out.

(939) Millie is a fan of Hailee Steinfeld.

(940) Millie thinks she can do a good cockney accent.

(941) Dazed wrote of meeting Millie in 2016 - 'The female staredown is back. Sultry, mesmerising, threatening, inscrutable, hungry: women giving good eye on screen literally inspires how we mirror emotion and communicate, whether through gif or IRL. The ferocious women of Kill Bill taught us that killer looks can prove fatal, Lauren Bacall pioneered the no-nonsense side-eye, and Rooney Mara's Lisbeth Salander made the chilling stare of a sniper seem chic. These steely-eyed women have a new little sister-in-arms: Eleven, the enigmatic, Eggo-pilfering, telekinetic dynamo from Stranger Things.

Portrayed by newcomer Millie Bobby Brown, her stare is genuinely enthralling, paralysing monsters – and boys – in their tracks. She reminds you of Natalie Portman in Leon or V for Vendetta – or a young Winona Ryder, with whom Brown stars in the series. She carries the onscreen gravitas of a future Oscar-winner, and the doe-eyed, gamine appeal of a budding fashion darling. Before we go any further, please note: she is 12 years old. Eleven is one of the most fascinating female characters ever to hit the small screen, embodying a twist on the coming-of-age stories that inspire Stranger Things.

In this universe, the classic boy-gang ends up rallying around a superhuman girl in an ultimate testament to their five-way friendship. After six months of shooting, the show wrapped, and the kids – including Finn Wolfhard, who plays Eleven's onscreen semi-crush Mike Wheeler – went about their normal lives, unaware that those were the last few normal months of their childhoods.'

(942) The comic books Max and Eleven are perusing in Stranger Things 3 are Wonder Woman #326, Wonder Woman #324, and Green Lantern #185.

(943) Some of the proceeds from Millie's makeup range go to the Olivia Hope Foundation. This was set up to honour Millie's late friend Olivia Hope LoRusso, who died following a 15-month battle with Acute Myeloid Leukemia. Millie raised

$40,000 for the Olivia Hope Foundation through Florence by Mills.

(944) Millie's career is very much a family affair. All of her relatives are part of the 'team' and have important roles.

(945) Millie said of making Enola Holmes in England - "I think just for me, I loved hearing the accent all day long, the banter, don't get me wrong I love working in America, but you know obviously home is home for me and I loved working with my people."

(946) When Eleven wears a bandana blindfold to make contact with Mike through the static of the television in Stranger Things 2, this is a reference to The Karate Kid.

(947) In an episode of The Simpsons, Homer watched a Stranger Things parody called Odder Stuff.

(948) Eleven is revealed to be a fan of Miami Vice in Stranger Things 3. This was a police action drama with Don Johnson broadcast on NBC from 1984 to 1989.

(949) Millie once danced with Harry Styles at an Ariana Grande concert.

(950) The Washington Post wrote of Enola Holmes - 'Millie Bobby Brown makes a high-spirited leading-role movie debut in Enola Holmes, which on paper might sound like a starchy exercise in feminist revisionism, but winds up executing that agenda with wit, pacey storytelling and an overarching mood of cracking good fun. Anchored by Brown's sturdy, self-possessed performance as Sherlock Holmes's teenage sister, this sprightly paean to mothers, daughters and female autonomy often feels like the spiritual sequel to last year's similarly lively "Little Women," albeit with more jokes, fight scenes and clever interstitial inserts thrown in for the viewer's enjoyment.

This rollicking Victorian-era adventure surely isn't canon, but the Baker Street Irregulars aren't its intended audience anyway. Arthur Conan Doyle might have created the universe in which "Enola Holmes" spins its flights of fancy, but that's where the similarity ends. Brown is surrounded by a superb ensemble of supporting players: Fiona Shaw brings her signature drollery to her role as a prissy finishing-school headmistress, and Claflin is amusingly fatuous as the insufferable Mycroft. But the movie succeeds or fails on her portrayal of a 16-year-old who has inherited the Holmes family brain (she's particularly gifted with unscrambling ciphers), but who's still naive in the ways of the world.

Brown plays that contradiction with unstudied ease, delivering dry asides to the camera with just the right amount of cheek, but never devolving into adorability for its own sake. She brings added warmth and game, understated grace to a movie that might begin to lag by the third act — at two hours and change, it feels unnecessarily long — but whose sunny disposition never falters. "Enola Holmes" offers brisk and exuberant escape from the heaviness of modern times, with its leading actress lending her own appealing touches to the journey. When the game is afoot, she's more than capable, not just of keeping up, but winning the day.'

(951) Millie said it never bothered her that her parents moved the family around a lot as children and they all got used to it quite quickly.

(952) On her fifteenth birthday, Millie took a lesson in making fresh pasta. She said she didn't quite get the hang of ravioli though.

(953) Millie said - "What I like about sci-fi and specifically that CGI element of our tech, and our movies, and TV, is that it really takes you into a different world. And especially during this time during the pandemic, it's been so stressful and scary. So watching something that can take you into a different world -- there's a calming effect to that. Things like animations... I

love things like that. It helps me just kind of immerse into a different world and feel like I'm not kind of having to deal with my own problems for a second."

(954) In 2017, The Hollywood Reporter wrote that Millie had overtaken Dwayne Johnson to become the most popular actor on social media. Data from Facebook, Instagram, Twitter, YouTube and Google Plus was used in the calculation.

(955) In 2018, The Hollywood Reporter named Millie as one of Hollywood's top thirty stars under the age of eighteen.

(956) Millie is a fan of Nutella chocolate spread. She likes eating it with breadsticks.

(957) Millie's father said - "My other children watched cartoons. Millie watched musicals – Chicago, Moulin Rouge, Annie and Bugsy Malone. She'd belt out a tune. She was performing from day one."

(958) The film producer Jonathan Southcott said in 2020 - "Millie's the real deal, she's at the top of everyone's radar. Her star is only going to soar."

(959) Godzilla v Kong seemed to get somewhat better reviews than Godzilla: King of the Monsters. The Guardian wrote - 'The humans are obviously of minimal importance (the finale in particular is jaw-droppingly callous in its destruction of an entire city and its inhabitants) but the script, from the Marvel writer Eric Pearson and the MonsterVerse stalwart Max Borenstein, uses the film's ensemble mostly well, they propel things along without dragging them down. There's no time for romance between Rebecca Hall's anthropological linguist and Alexander Skarsgård's geologist or between Millie Bobby Brown's Godzilla-stanning teen and her friend Julian Dennison and while Brian Tyree Henry's conspiracy theorist podcaster does get lumped with comic support, it's breezy enough not to get annoying. The most impactful human character is played by deaf actor Kaylee Hottle, playing a girl

who shares a bond with Kong, whose scenes come closest to giving the film some sort of heart. But ultimately it works best when operating on the grandest scale imaginable and while there's a bittersweet tinge for those of us watching it at home, it's already serving as a reminder why the big screen experience will never go away.'

(960) Millie said she can't believe how tiny and young she looks in the first season of Stranger Things. It seems like a very long time ago to her now.

(961) According to Hype Editor, as of 2021, Millie is the 33rd most followed person on Instagram in the world.

(962) Linnea Berthelsen was cast as Kali in Stranger Things 2 on the recommendation of Millie. Millie watched some of the auditions and told the Duffers that Berthelsen was very good.

(963) Although she appeared in Grey's Anatomy, Millie said she has never actually watched the show.

(964) In season one and two of stranger Things, Hopper wears the hairband of his late daughter Sarah on his wrist. From the finale of season two onwards, Eleven wears this hairband on her wrist.

(965) TIME magazine said of Stranger Things 3 that - 'The more permanent paradigm shifts of this season not only offer audiences a number of powerful dramatic moments, but it also sets the stage for an entirely new dynamic in whatever comes next while also concluding this journey in a fulfilling way that doesn't actually require another season. After having spent three years with these characters, these revelations feel fully earned, all while reminding both the audience and the characters that you can never go back to merely sitting in your basement playing D&D, no matter how much joy that would bring you.'

(966) Millie likes using pillow mist. Pillow mist produces

aromas which are said to induce sleep.

(967) Shawn Levy played the Stranger Things score from seasons one and two on the set of The Sauna Test to get Millie and the young cast members in the right mood for their confrontation with the possessed Billy Hargrove.

(968) Millie is fond of raspberry lipstick.

(969) Millie said she pranked the Duffers on season one of Stranger Things by filling her mouth with water and pretending she was sick and vomiting.

(970) Millie said she is a fan of the Pixar film Inside Out.

(971) The word 'telekinesis' was first used in 1890 by Russian psychical researcher Alexander N. Aksakof.

(972) In 2016, Netflix released the results of a study based on its subscriber data which sought to deduce how many episodes it took viewers to get hooked on a variety of televisions shows. According to this specific data, the first season of Stranger Things took three episodes to completely hook the viewer into watching the rest.

(973) The Provision Coffee Bar in Phoenix celebrated Halloween in 2019 with a Stranger Things cocktail they named the Eleven. The drink was served with a mini Eggo waffle.

(974) Finn Wolfhard says he enjoys the 'awkward' romance of Mike and Eleven in Stranger Things. Millie begged to differ though and said she didn't think the romance was awkward.

(975) A photo of Eleven from Stranger Things that has been personally signed by Millie can sell for over $400 on the net.

(976) Millie said of shooting Stranger Things 3 - "You know the scenes where it looks like I'm falling? I had to learn how to basically throw myself backwards and forwards for a few

hours. And by the end of it, I was gagging because I was so nauseous, but it was the best. I loved it, I loved every second of it. But yes, stunt-wise, it was quite difficult this year."

(977) During the production of a new season of Stranger Things, they carefully monitor the frequency and nature of Eleven's nosebleeds in past episodes to make sure they remain consistent depicting her nosebleeds in the new episodes.

(978) The first time Millie had a sleepover at Maddie Ziegler's house, a fire alarm went off at 3am and they had to evacuate the house. Firefighters even turned up (although thankfully there was no fire).

(979) Millie has a few freckles on one of her cheeks.

(980) The candy store It'Sugar offered some Stranger Things themed treats by creating Gummy Eggos.

(981) Millie said that when she used to attend auditions as an aspiring child actor her father wouldn't take her to an audition unless she knew her lines. This was a pragmatic time and money saving tactic. Millie's father wanted to make a priority of the auditions that she was best prepared for and had the best chance of being hired.

(982) Millie said that because her family experienced financial hardships trying to support her acting ambitions she appreciates the comfortable lifestyle she has now all the more. She doesn't take it for granted.

(983) Millie said she is quite interested in astrology and the zodiac.

(984) Stranger Things seems inspired in part by the 1980 Ken Russell film Altered States - which also features sensory deprivation experiments.

(985) In numerology, the number Eleven is symbolic of the

potential to push the limitations of the human experience into the stratosphere of the highest spiritual perception; the link between the mortal and the immortal; between man and spirit; between darkness and light; ignorance and enlightenment.

(986) Talent manager Jonathan Shalit said of Millie - "Being nominated for an Emmy at 13 set her on an incredible path. There's no actress in the world who is as compelling as Millie. Her humility and honesty shine."

(987) Stranger Things casting director Carmen Cuba said - "Training and/or life experience teaches adults how to leave some of their quirks off the table. But kids are mostly unable to cover up the things that make them uniquely who they are — and I love that."

(988) Millie seems to be a fan of the bucket hat.

(989) The Indian Express wrote of Enola Holmes - 'The Sherlock universe is already well populated, with the likes of Robert Downey Jr, Benedict Cumberbatch having donned the famous ear-flapped travelling cap, and who can forget Johnny Lee Miller in the Elementary with Lucy Lui as Joan Watson, upending gender in the police procedural show. House MD too was inspired by Sherlock Holmes. With Enola Holmes, we are taken into that universe yet again, and its a pleasant surprise. We meet a Sherlock who speaks less, is happy to play second fiddle to his younger sister and is downright proud of her achievements.

The lack of a super-sized ego and arrogance took some getting used to, but that's what David Bradbeer, the director was going for. This is where Enola Holmes goes beyond Elementary. Its all about Enola, as she gets into scrapes, breaks the fourth wall with charming alacrity — hello Fleabag, David Bardbeer directed Fleabag as well — and forges her own path. Phoebe Waller-Bridge has inspired this trend of speaking to the audience directly, and we couldn't be happier.

Her path entwines with the young Viscount of Tweaksbury, a dashing Marquess to be, and oh, yes there is an all-important vote that will be held in the House of Lords. The scenes between Enola and Sherlock — obviously he has her favour, unlike the stoogey Mycroft — are the best in the film, as he comes to recognise her as an equal and a force to be reckoned with, instead of the young smock wearing girl. Has Sherlock gone soft in his latest avatar? Well, we are not complaining. We have not had a strong female detective in a while, and Agatha Christie's Miss Marple seems a long time ago. Millie Bobby Brown, fresh from the success of Netflix's Stranger Things, is the perfect casting for a quirky Enola, and Henry Cavill with his perfectly wavy hair is enigmatic enough to play Sherlock.'

(990) Millie is set to star in a new Netflix fantasy film called Damsel. In Damsel, Millie will play Princess Elodie, who thinks she is marrying Prince Henry, only to find out that she is being sacrificed to a dragon.

(991) Millie is a fan of Coach fashion.

(992) The Duffer Brothers think that because the kids in the cast are growing up fast, this is good because it means Stranger Things will feel different each time it returns. "It forces the show to evolve and change, because the kids are changing. Even if we wanted it to be static and we wanted to continually recycle the same storyline — and we don't — we would be unable to, just because the kids are changing. It's cool, though. The audience is going to be able to watch these kids come of age every year. The closest example is Harry Potter. Watching those kids and actors grow up in front of the camera was, to me, very powerful."

(993) Although she was born in Spain, Millie doesn't speak much Spanish. Because her family were English no one spoke any Spanish at home.

(994) Fancasting websites (in which they suggest famous roles for actors to play) have suggested that Millie would be good as Shadowcat or Squirrel Girlin the Marvel universe, Dorothy in The Wizard of Oz, Wendy in Peter Pan, and (of course) Princess Leia in Star Wars.

(995) Millie is a fan of doughnuts. In America they would says donuts.

(996) Stranger Things become a huge phenomenon through word of mouth and positive reviews. Film websites like Badass Digest and Ain't It Cool urged their readers to watch Stranger Things. Stephen King and Steven Spielberg raved about the show. The positive buzz for the show grew and grew. Stranger Things was by some distance the big TV success of the year in 2016. The Duffers and Shawn Levy could hardly believe how popular Stranger Things had proved to be. They knew the show was good but they never dreamed it would have such mass appeal. Most people thought that binging all eight episodes of Stranger Things in 2016 was much more fun than watching the latest Hollywood blockbusters.

(997) Millie said the boys in Stranger Things drove her "loopy" a few times when they were shooting season one.

(998) Millie said she usually starts the day with a cup of tea.

(999) Millie is what you might describe as a self-made actor and celebrity. She had none of the advantages that many in her profession enjoy. She was not a Disney factory kid, her parents were not actors or directors, she didn't go to any talent schools, she has never been in any theatrical productions on the stage, she isn't from Hollywood, and her family were far from rich.

(1000) Because she had all but given up on her acting career at one point, Millie says that everything that has happened since 2016 feels like a dream.

Lightning Source UK Ltd.
Milton Keynes UK
UKHW040831250522
403501UK00002B/58